Billy Graham

A LIFE IN PICTURES

KEN GARFIELD

TRIUMPH
BOOKS

TRIUMPHBOOKS.COM

Billy Graham A LIFE IN PICTURES

AP PHOTO/JEFFREY HADERTHAUER

Rev. Billy Graham preaching in Oklahoma City, June 15, 2003.

Author:
Ken Garfield

Photography:
A.P. Photos, Todd Sumlin,
*The Charlotte Observer, The Kansas
City Star, The Philadelphia Inquirer*

Designer:
Andrea Ware

This book is a joint production of
Triumph Books LLC and
The McClatchy Company.

Triumph Books LLC
814 N. Franklin St.reet
Chicago, Illinois 60610
(800) 888-4741
Fax (312) 337-1807

Printed in the United States of America

ISBN: 978-1-57243-581-0

Ken Garfield is former religion editor of *The Charlotte* (N.C.) *Observer*, having supervised coverage of faith in the Carolinas for the region's largest newspaper for 12 years. In addition to overseeing the paper's weekly Faith & Values section, he wrote six columns a month on faith and family, hosted a weekly show on Christian radio and was a frequent speaker at church and civic meetings. He is now director of communications at 5,100-member Myers Park United Methodist Church. He and his wife, Sharon, have two children, Matthew and Ellen, and live in Charlotte.

CONTENTS

ACKNOWLEDGMENTS

In more than a decade of covering religion for *The Charlotte Observer*, I was blessed to meet some unforgettable people who made their marks on the world.

I have received prayer beads from Mother Teresa during her visit to Charlotte, which I keep now in a safe place on my desk, near my Bible. I have been warmed by the smile of the Tibetan Buddhist leader Dalai Lama, a gentle man of peace whose people were victimized by Chinese political oppression. I have laughed at the childlike energy of those wacky TV evangelists of old, Jim and Tammy Bakker.

But I never met anyone like Billy Graham.

I consider it a rare privilege to have known and written about the man who changed the face of modern Christianity, and changed who knows how many lives over the course of a ministry that has spanned more than 50 years.

I watched him enthrall 250,000 New Yorkers at a rally

Ken Garfield with Billy Graham.

on a sunny afternoon in New York's Central Park. (He even drew more applause than Kathie Lee Gifford, the TV talk show host and ardent Christian who sang at the rally.) I listened as he spoke in a small hall in the industrial town of Essen, preaching gently to elderly Germans still haunted by their nation's role in the horrors of war. I was there at then brand-new Ericsson Stadium in his native Charlotte as he preached to more than 300,000 at a buoyant Carolinas homecoming. I fought the wind in 1998 at Raymond James Stadium in Tampa, Fla., as he celebrated his 80th birthday doing what he has always done. Standing on a giant platform, sharing the joy of Jesus with those who know the feeling and those who might not.

Late in life, when he'd make a rare public appearance here in his hometown, he'd find a moment for me. We'd shake hands warmly, he'd smile broadly and we'd share a kind word before his handlers and the masses pulled him away. A framed photograph of each visit graces a wall of my home. We both aged from one photo to the next.

At each stop along the way, I have been awed by Graham's power, moved by his gentleness and touched by the courage it took to grow old on a stage he steadfastly refused to exit.

In these next few pages filled with words, photographs and memories, it is an honor to be able to share with you the Billy Graham I know.

My goal is simple — to help you appreciate anew the impact and humanity of a man who could transfix great crowds one day and then go home quietly to the Western North Carolina mountains the next to be a husband, father and friend.

Who was he? Where did he come from? What did he mean to the world?

Together, we'll consider the answers.

There are so many people to thank for the privilege I've been given here:

The good people of Triumph Books, who saw the need to honor Billy Graham with this work.

All the editors and publishers, past and present, at *The Charlotte Observer* who drew me to the religion beat and then sustained me with their counsel and support: Frank Barrows, Cheryl Carpenter, Ann Caulkins, Cindy Montgomery, Rolfe Neill, Rich Oppel, Peter Ridder, Greg Ring, Rick Thames and Jim Walser to name some but not nearly all.

The aides, publicists and spokespersons who served for years as gentle intermediaries between Graham and the press, especially Larry Ross, Mark DeMoss, Jeremy Blume, David Bruce and Merrell Gregory. When you've shared meals and conversation all over the world with people, they become more than acquaintances.

The Grahams' official photographer (and my pal), Russ Busby, who never went anywhere in the world without his camera and a passion for using it to record history.

The scholars who put it all into context for me and so many others, including Graham biographer William Martin and historian Grant Wacker. Their approach to all this is a perfect blend of intellect and wonder.

The Graham kinfolk who were always there with a smile and a word about how Billy and his late-wife, Ruth, were doing. I smile when I think of his late brother Melvin, sister Jean and her husband, Leighton Ford. Franklin Graham of Boone, N.C., and Anne Graham Lotz of Raleigh, the two most prominent Graham children, had the added burden of being public figures.

The other religion writers around the nation, past and present, who shared their wisdom and humor on the road to the best stories, including Gayle White in Atlanta, John Railey in Winston-Salem, N.C., Judith Cebula in Indianapolis, Mark Pinsky in Orlando, Cary McMullen in Lakeland, Fla., Abe Levy in Wichita, Kan., and Susan Hogan/Albach and Berta Delgado in Dallas. We all shared a Graham story or two along the way.

Finally — first, actually — I thank my family:

My late, beloved parents, Sam and Jean, for raising me to keep an open mind, a feeling heart and an appreciation for God in any form.

Our children, Matthew and Ellen, for teaching us a thing or two about what it means to be devoted.

And my wife, Sharon, most of all, who said a loving good-bye each time I headed out to a Billy Graham event and a joyful hello when I came back home with a rich, new story to tell.

— Ken Garfield

1991

Preaching in 1996.

MEASURING THE MAN

Celebrating the life and times of Billy Graham takes many forms.

The close-knit Graham family considers him a beloved patriarch, a gentle man who approaches the end of his long life with a quiet gratitude and graceful acceptance. He has always said he is ready to go when the Lord is ready to take him. No surprise there. He put his life in the Lord's hands; why wouldn't he do the same when the time comes?

More than a pulpiteer, the world lifts up a leader who was frequently called on to pray over the years with the powerful and soothe the frightened. The first President George Bush summoned him to the White House for prayer before the Desert Storm offensive against Iraq in 1991. The second President George Bush, who once lived hard and admittedly drank more than he should, came to his quiet, serious faith through Billy Graham. When America needed to hear unifying words of reflection after the Oklahoma City bombing of 1995, there was no doubt about who to summon for a nationally televised memorial service.

But honoring him goes deeper.

Christianity considers him one of its most influential ambassadors, along with Mother Teresa surely the most universally admired messenger of any faith in modern times. If the worst you can say about a public figure is he had too much influence over the rich and famous — as Graham's critics argued he did — then that's a pretty fair lifetime's work.

And the world affirms a man whose reach can, in fact, be measured: In more than 50 years of ministry, this evangelist raised on a dairy farm in Charlotte, N.C., preached to more than 210 million people in 185 countries and territories. More than 15.5 million copies of his various books have been sold in 38 lan-

The world honors a man whose reach can, in fact, be measured: In more than 50 years of ministry, this evangelist raised on a dairy farm in Charlotte, N.C., preached to more than 210 million people in 185 countries and territories.

Billy Graham's boyhood home in Charlotte, N.C.

1992 portrait.

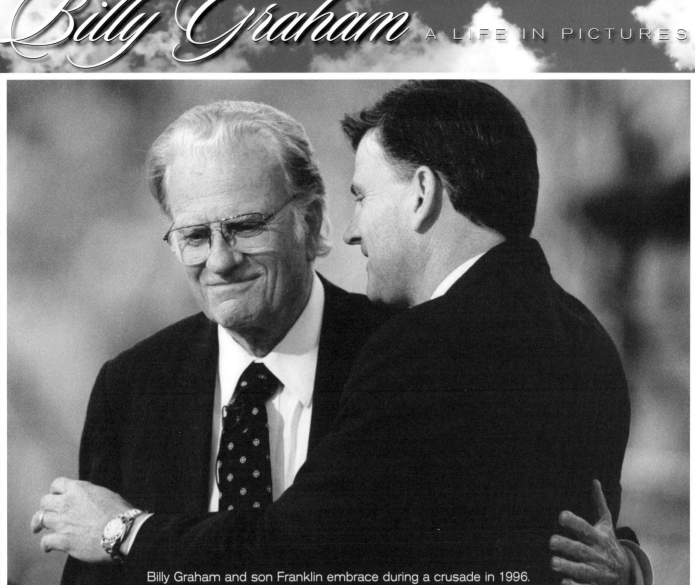

Billy Graham and son Franklin embrace during a crusade in 1996.

AP PHOTO/PETER A. HARRIS

guages worldwide. In one day alone in 1973 in Seoul, South Korea, he spoke of the saving power of Jesus to more than 1.1 million people. All the pastors in almost any American city could add up all the people to whom they have preached in a lifetime and it wouldn't match that matchless number.

His reach was such that people could mail handwritten pleas for prayer addressed to "Billy Graham, Many Apples, U.S.A.," and it would reach him at his ministry's former headquarters — in downtown Minneapolis, U.S.A. at the time.

But as staggering and inspiring as this all is, there is more.

THE CHARLOTTE OBSERVER

Overflow crowd at Billy Graham's 1996 crusade in Charlotte, N.C.

THE CHARLOTTE OBSERVER

Chronicling the dimensions of his impact must consider also the legacy of a man whose achievements will live on and on, long after the mention of a Billy Graham crusade takes us back to another era long, long ago.

What Billy Graham accomplished will never fade from the modern religious landscape, even as his work goes on.

He shows us what it means to embrace a faith, and then stick with it until the end, without changing the message or how he presented it. As we shall see later, early on in his ministry he decided never to bow to the intellectuals and question his belief that God will accept us if we accept Him. It was so simple, so basic a belief that even cynics and doubters could be moved to believe themselves.

He shows us what it means to sacrifice for the privilege of sharing your faith. The temptation to stay home in North Carolina and raise a family was powerful. He spoke often earlier in his career, with lament,

His reach is such that people could mail handwritten pleas for prayer addressed to "Billy Graham, Many Apples, U.S.A.," and it would reach him at his ministry's former headquarters — in downtown Minneapolis, U.S.A. at the time.

Graham in 1996.

Graham in 1989 in the library of his offices in Montreat, N.C.

Billy Graham and son Franklin in Raleigh in 1994.

of playing the role of preacher while forcing Ruth to play the more challenging role of both mother and father.

It isn't easy; great work never is. The story goes that one of the Grahams' five children once found their mother and father in bed together and asked who that strange man was sleeping with Mama. The stranger in his own home sacrificed being a father so he could be a traveling evangelist. Truth be told, in his later years, Graham would just as soon have sat at home in his easy chair in Montreat in the mountains,

beside his wife, Ruth, wrestling over the remote control.

But the pull to parenthood, the pull to live the normal life of a father, husband and retired preacher, was not as powerful as living up to the responsibility he felt God had laid on him over the years — to go out and preach the Gospel.

He shows us that it's possible to be influential, famous and honest — no easy accomplishment in a religious world populated by con men and quacks.

He lives a modest lifestyle in a simple log home, never having sur-

He shows us that it's possible to be influential, famous and honest — no easy accomplishment in a religious world populated by con men and quacks.

rendered to a lust for lavishness. He was a faithful husband; the famous Billy sraham rule was that he never entered a room alone with another woman. His ministry remains as financially chaste as the man who ran it, never pushing too hard for money from supporters and never misusing what it receives. A set of rules adopted with his allies one day early in his ministry in Modesto, Calif. — the Modesto Manifesto it was called — became his personal Bible of integrity. The way he lives his life each day speaks as powerfully as his words.

Like no other religious figure, Billy Graham has harnessed technol-ogy for the good.

Those who couldn't hear him in person could find so many other paths that led to Graham, and to faith:

More than 100 million people have seen at least one of the Christian movies produced by his ministry. More than 70 million have received at least one copy of one of his sermons, mailed free to your home. His newspaper col-umn reaches 5 million readers. His *Decision* magazine, still going strong, reaches subscribers in more than 150 countries. More than 700 stations at one time carried his trademark *Hour of Decision* radio program. How many of us dressed for church, listening to Graham preach to us over the radio?

Like clockwork, Graham would hold a crusade — then profession-ally produced highlights of that crusade would air on syndicated television in cities across America. On one station, you'd find the latest reality TV nonsense. On the other, Graham would buy time with the station so he could exhort those on the fence to come forward and commit their lives to Christ. As they made their walk to faith, the mass choir chosen from the community just for this special occasion sang "Just As I Am" behind him.

Leighton Ford.

MARK B. SLUDER/THE CHARLOTTE OBSERVER

that nearly took him several times, Graham kept preaching into his 90s. Parkinson's disease robbed him of his balance. Fluid on the brain nearly killed him. Old age saps his vigor. A bit of martyrdom always left him with a malady to talk about. His brother-in-law, evangelist Leighton Ford of Charlotte, joked through the years that resolute Ruth Bell Graham's tombstone would read, "Never Felt Better." Billy's will read, "I Told You So!"

> *This may be Graham's greatest legacy: He took the church and brought it into modern times.*

Despite aches and pains and old age, though, he kept on scheduling crusades at least until a few years ago, even if he sometimes had to sit down in the middle of a stem-winder of a sermon.

I remember watching him preach at Raymond James Stadium in Tampa, Fla., in October 1998, just as he was turning 80. The wind was blowing hard that unseasonably cold October night. I watched the massive scaffolding weighed down by stage lights shake in the breeze above Graham. I remember him gripping the pulpit tighter than

This wasn't just a smart organization figuring out how to spread the word. This was spiritual genius at work — understanding that to save the world, you had to reach the world by going outside the church and into homes in every way possible. This may be Graham's greatest legacy years from now: He took the church and brought it into modern times.

There is more.

Graham strengthens the local church. Unlike so many other evangelists who seek to win people only to his or her ministry, Graham's aim is to funnel people back to a congregation. You find inspiration at a Graham crusade. Graham believes you find a lifetime of support and fellowship in a congregation of your choice.

He personifies courage.

Through accidents and illness

This was spiritual genius at work — understanding that to save the world, you had to reach the world by going outside the church and into homes in every way possible. This may be Graham's greatest legacy: He took the church and brought it into modern times.

TODD SUMLIN/THE CHARLOTTE OBSERVER

2002

usual, holding on against the wind.

But mostly what I remember is the silver-haired evangelist plowing ahead, as always, thinking not of himself but of the message he yearned to share.

Plowing ahead with courage, thinking of others first. A pretty fair lesson to deliver to the fragile, the fearful and the old.

There have been missteps, to which even Graham confessed.

He allowed himself to be sucked in by politics and power, leaving the impression with some that he spoke only for the rich and the Republicans. He stayed largely silent on the Vietnam War, and became a sounding board and sympathizer for Richard Nixon. Late in his life, he had to apologize for anti-Semitic comments he made to that disgraced President that had been caught for all time on tape.

In print once, *Washington Post* columnist Edwin M. Yoder Jr. called Graham "the companion and comforter of the mighty…"

Graham agreed — "I went too far," he said in 1993, long after Watergate had shattered his faith in Nixon, and much about politics. "I should have limited myself to the moral and spiritual situation in the country." He did so later in life, refusing to endorse old friend George Bush for the presidency in 1992, and refusing to publicly pass judgment on President Clinton's sexual misconduct.

But such criticism and confession seems like ancient history.

As we'll explore here, what matters is that a man was born and raised on a dairy farm in North

1986 in Charlotte, N.C.

JOE EDENS/THE CHARLOTTE OBSERVER

CHARLOTTE OBSERVER FILE PHOTO

Carolina.

His faith blossomed at a country revival.

He married a woman who became the world to him.

He decided never to question his beliefs about God.

He set out to save the world for Christ.

He achieved recognition and respect.

He overcame illness.

He softened and broadened his message with age.

He succeeded like no one ever has. And surely no one ever will.

The Graham dairy farm.

ROAD TO A REVIVAL

Who could have imagined that a gangly farm boy from a small North Carolina town would grow up to become modern times' most famous religious figure?

Not Jim Stenhouse of Charlotte, N.C., a prominent architect who first knew Graham as the youngster who hauled milk to his door at Eighth and Pine Streets in 1926, at the impressionable age of eight.

"He was just a kid," Stenhouse said only months before he passed away in 1996 at age 86. "He was just the kid who drove the milk wagon. I had no idea he'd be what he is."

Neither did the milkman-turned-evangelist, whose life revolved around what most every Southern boy's life revolved around way back when: Baseball, girls, bicycles, boys' adventure books, goats, mules, cows, horseshoes, the magic of the radio, working in his mother's garden — the stuff of good, simple, honest living

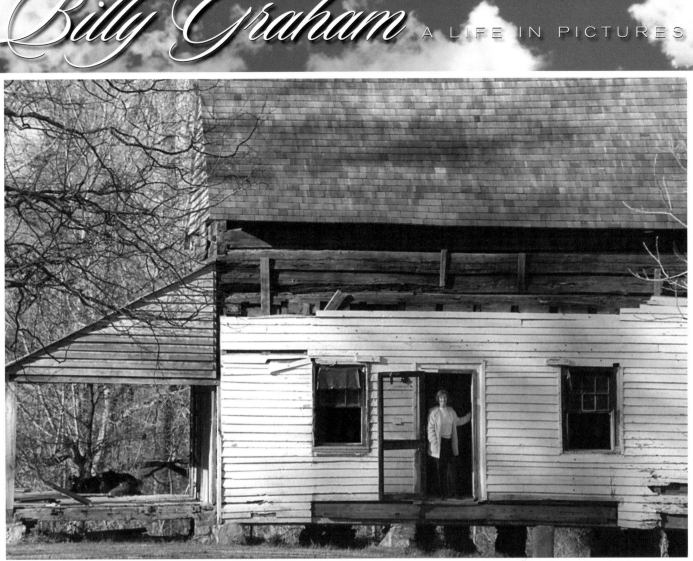

Debbie Matthews, Grants and Donations Coordinator for Anne Springs Close Greenway, stands in the doorway of a 1780 log cabin that was once home to the Rev. Billy Graham's grandfather.

DIEDRA LAIRD/THE CHARLOTTE OBSERVER

that served him well when he rose to a life of faith and glory.

There's a lesson here, of course.

Like so many men and women who changed the world, Graham wasn't raised to be famous or influential; he didn't plot to gain power; he didn't ache at an early age to be anything but what he was — a normal boy brought up in a good, modest, loving home.

The greatness, and the impact, came to him naturally.

Did it come to Billy Graham because he was touched by God?

Because he was in the right place at the right time when the world

Like so many men and women who changed the world, Graham wasn't raised to be famous or influential; he didn't plot to gain power; he didn't ache at an early age to be anything but what he was — a normal boy brought up in a good, modest, loving home.

1

needed an uncompromising Christian evangelist?

Or was it a blend of both?

Each of us must answer that question for ourselves, based on what we believe.

But whatever the reason for the rise of Billy Graham, the modesty with which he was born stayed with him as the world's spotlight turned his way.

Isn't it like that for the truly great souls among us? They don't demand our attention. But when they get it, we are the better for it.

William Morrow Graham was born on Nov. 7, 1918, to Charlotte dairy farmers William Franklin and Morrow Coffey Graham. It was four days before the armistice that ended World War I, and he came into the world in the family's farmhouse, a white, frame home with green trim overlooking pastures filled with the Graham herd of cattle.

Today?

That farm is a shopping center on a busy road in the heart of the Carolinas' largest city. A multiplex movie theater, an upscale sports bar/restaurant and a wine superstore dominate a corner of the world that once held another kind of wealth — wide, open spaces.

His parents were descendants of Scottish pioneers — ardent Presbyterians who raised their children to work hard, pray often and live sparely. Indulgence in the Graham household meant piling into the family car on a Saturday night and driving to a nearby country store or to Niven's Drugstore downtown for a soda or ice cream cone. Or maybe taking a trip to Myrtle Beach, Wilmington or Magnolia Gardens near Charleston.

Each day, young Billy milked a lot of Guernseys, 20 he recalled decades later. He remembers the hours he spent milking those cows — plus the shoveling of hay and manure that went with it. The sound of the alarm clock going off at 2:30 a.m., signaling another day of work, never faded from his memory.

He attributed the C's he regularly earned at Sharon High School to life on the farm. Who had time and energy to study when there were cows to milk and gardens to cultivate?

By night, his button-down father read Scripture to Graham and his brother and sisters, Catherine, Melvin

The graduating class of the Beginners' Department at Chalmers Memorial ARP Meeting House in 1924. Evangelist Billy Graham is second from left.

SHARON HIGH SCHOOL'S GRADUATING CLASS

Billy Graham is in the third row, fourth from the left.

and Jean — a sliver of faith from his childhood that came into his heart early and never left.

"My mother was a great woman of God," Graham recalled. "My father, he could barely read and write. But he could read the Bible. People would come from miles around just to hear him tell jokes and stories."

Graham smiles easily when he reminisces. Over the years, he'd answer questions about kings and queens and crusades and presidents. But he seems to savor most deeply those moments that carry him back to another time. You can almost see him breathe in the memories and try

At six months old with his mother, Morrow, at the family farm.

not to let them out.

"It's the little things that come back," he told me, recalling during one of our visits an elderly black man

named Sam who used to preach to the kids about right and wrong as he drove their school bus. "Maybe they're the most important in God's sight."

The Grahams attended Chalmers Memorial Associate Reformed Presbyterian Meeting House in what is now an upscale neighborhood filled with funky bars and fancy steakhouses. Back then, in the 1920s, it was a crossroads where the Grahams went to make sure their children were raised right.

He remembers his mother making him memorize the Westminster Presbyterian catechism before he was 10. But he remembers so much more than those first hours devoted to God.

He loved the family collies, cats and goats that always populated the farm. He devoured the Tarzan series of books, plus the Tom Swift and Rover Boys adventures. The kid could do a pretty fair Tarzan yell, which especially delighted his sister, Catherine.

His buddy for life was his kid brother by six years, Melvin, who stayed on a farm in Matthews, N.C. all the years his big brother traveled the world preaching. If Billy was the serious one, Melvin, who preceded his brother in death, was always the card with the dapper cap covering his long, gray hair, telling a story and laughing at the punch line. The best part of my day was calling Melvin somewhere in his barn or on his farm. The sweet fellow would always drop what he was doing to chat about this or that. He was more than affable, though: He was an accomplished businessman and evangelist in his own right, speaking often to church groups about his family and faith.

Growing up as Billy did in a Christian home in the rural South of the early 20th Century, there was no drinking, of course. His father forced him and sister Catherine to each drink a beer one night in the kitchen. They were 15. The wise father knew they'd hate it enough to turn it down when their friends tried to tempt them as teenage friends did even way back when. He also gave Billy a

DAVIE HINSHAW/THE CHARLOTTE OBSERVER

Melvin Graham in 1997.

Graham preaching in front of the U.S. Capitol in Washington, Feb. 3, 1952.

AP WORLD WIDE PHOTOS

CHARLOTTE OBSERVER FILE PHOTO

Graham at age 19.

whipping the one time he found him with a chew of tobacco in his mouth.

Girls?

Billy liked classmate Jeanne Elliott, but only as a pal. And he never went beyond holding hands and the occasional stolen kiss, despite admitting to the usual case of adolescent hormones. Generally, though, he'd just as soon have been playing his beloved baseball as chasing someone of the opposite sex.

Rather than dreaming of girls, or even of commanding a pulpit in some faraway land, Billy dreamed of hitting homers for his beloved Philadelphia Athletics.

This was a good life in simpler times in the quiet South, where there was no glimmer of what lay ahead for this lanky young son of a dairy farmer.

Until one autumn night in 1934.

There are many ways to meet the Lord.

For some, the long journey is fraught with thinking, reading, worrying and praying. It's a process more than a revelation.

For others, it's a lightning bolt out of the blue. Christians who have the experience speak of being born again — a single instant in their life when they believe Christ came into their hearts. They can tell you the date and time, how they felt their heart pound or their eyes open wide. They knew what it was, and they knew then their lives would never be the same.

For Billy Graham, the leap of faith that has lasted a lifetime didn't come

DAVIE HINSHAW/THE CHARLOTTE OBSERVER

Melvin Graham in 1997.

Preaching in 1986.

JOE EDENS/THE CHARLOTTE OBSERVER

at the end of a long journey or as a sudden thunderclap from the heavens.

It came with a simple, quiet, deliberate decision made by a 16-year-old boy who calmly stepped forward and never stepped back. Not many teenagers found Christ that way, then stuck by Him. It seems appropriate that this one young man took a path taken by so few.

Dr. Mordecai Fowler Ham was coming to town.

Then, as now, Charlotte had the reputation for being a church-going city, a place where a fiery evangelist like Ham could stir the masses. A balding, well-dressed man with a white mustache and eyeglasses, Ham was invited by the Christian Men's Club, which had been organized

For Billy Graham, the leap of faith that has lasted a lifetime didn't come at the end of a long journey or as a sudden thunderclap from the heavens. It came with a simple, quiet, deliberate decision made by a 16-year-old boy who calmly stepped forward and never stepped back.

in 1924 in Charlotte after a revival by traveling evangelist Billy Sunday, another fire-breather of his day.

Ham, a Southern Baptist preacher and former traveling sales-man, was to preach six days a week

Mr. & Mrs. Billy Graham in 1955.

Billy Graham reading on his porch in Montreat in 1966.

for 11 weeks in a tabernacle built for the occasion on Pecan Avenue. Sawdust covered the floor.

At first, Graham wasn't especially interested in attending Ham's revival. Graham had been baptized, confirmed and raised in the church, and obediently listened to his parents regularly read the Bible aloud. But he was an indifferent believer at this point, not unlike many boys who had other things on their mind. One day at vacation Bible school, Graham heaved a Bible across the room, much to the annoyance of his teacher. That pretty well summed up the spiritual depth of the baseball-loving farm boy.

At first, Graham stubbornly stayed away from Ham's meetings, despite his parents' enthusiasm for the special event. But then he read in the local newspaper that Ham had accused students at Central High in Charlotte of engaging in immoral activities. When rumors began to spread of a student protest in response, curiosity won out.

Graham entered the tabernacle, taking a seat in the back to see what might happen.

Graham couldn't recall exactly what Ham talked about that first night. But he distinctly remembered being spellbound, as if someone even more powerful than this man was talking directly to him. He returned the next night, and for many nights after that, magnetized by this preacher warning people to

get right with God or suffer the consequences of eternal damnation.

One night, Graham tried to hide behind the wide-brimmed hat of the lady in front of him, so sure that Ham was directing his tirade against sin right at him. Not even joining the choir, so he could sit behind Ham and out of his line of fire, could keep Graham from absorbing the full force of Ham's attack.

He finally surrendered.

As Ham invited people to come forward at the end of the service and turn their lives over to Christ — the pivotal moment of the evangelical Christian experience — the choir began to sing "Almost Persuaded, Now to Believe." On

Billy Graham at the site of his birth, in 1973.

the last verse, Graham got up out of his chair and walked to the front. He doesn't know precisely why he did it, he just did.

There were no tears, much as he wanted to be rocked by emotion that night. He didn't tremble. His heart didn't beat any faster than it usually did. He remembered a family friend putting his arm around him and weeping, but it wasn't anything earth-shattering.

Graham simply checked "Recommitment" on the card that Ham asked people to fill out. Then he went home to be commended by his mother and father.

And yet, despite the ordinary trappings of the occasion, Graham remembers the feeling of being

completely changed the day he answered that altar call. It was as if he had turned a corner without the possibility of looking back.

Simple as that.

"All I knew is that the world looked different the next morning when I got up to do the milking, eat breakfast, and catch the school bus," Graham wrote years later in his autobiography, "There seemed to be a song in my heart...."

The road to the pulpit was filled with other important stops for Graham.

He was baptized in Palatka, Fla., while studying at Florida Bible Institute. That's where he refined his delivery and style — preaching to the wildlife in a Florida swamp. He

graduated from Wheaton College in Illinois, where he met the second most important figure in his life after Christ — a missionary's daughter, Ruth McCue Bell, whom he married in 1943 in Montreat. He began his rise to glory preaching with Youth for Christ in Chicago.

But none of it would have mattered for all time if curiosity hadn't gotten the best of him.

If he hadn't walked tentatively into a tabernacle that autumn night in 1934 in his hometown to hear Mordecai Ham.

If he hadn't heard the Lord speaking to him through a silver-tongued evangelist.

If he hadn't heard a song in his heart.

Graham with Johnny Cash in 1991.

A DECISION BY A ROCK

Just as he dedicated his life to Christ in one swift moment at a Mordecai Ham revival in his hometown of Charlotte on an autumn night in 1934, Billy Graham laid all doubts aside on a summer's night in 1949.

It took place under the California stars, and it was part of an undeniable pattern in his life: One fundamental decision, made with little doubt or hesitation, blossoming into a lifetime of leading others down the same path.

It's easy to look back now and pick out the half-dozen or so moments that shape any life into what it eventually becomes. It's even easier to do that with the lives of people for whom those moments became springboards to greatness.

A simple bronze tablet beside a stone in the San Bernardino Mountains outside Los Angeles marks the spot of just such a springboard.

It was August of 1949, and Graham had come to the Forest

Home retreat center in southern California to lead a student conference with fellow Youth for Christ evangelist Charles Templeton. By the time the two fast-rising evangelists had come west to do their thing, Graham had already climbed onto the evangelical fast track.

On so many fronts both professional and personal, he was moving swiftly in the right direction:

He had graduated from Florida Bible Institute in 1940, perfecting his oratorical skills first by himself in a swamp and then at tiny Bostwick Baptist Church around 1937 in the north Florida town of Bostwick.

Today, who outside of Florida even knows of this place that played a part in religious history?

The exact date of Graham's moment in Bostwick has become clouded by the passing of time. But years later, Graham could recount that night in Bostwick as if it were yesterday. The details of pivotal moments never leave us, do they?

Graham remembered the potbellied iron stove near the front of the small church, the main source of warmth for those often chilly nights in north Florida.

He remembered the song leader who had to excuse himself to go

Just as he dedicated his life to Christ in one swift moment at a Mordecai Ham revival in his hometown of Charlotte on an autumn night in 1934, Billy Graham laid all doubts aside on a summer's night in 1949.

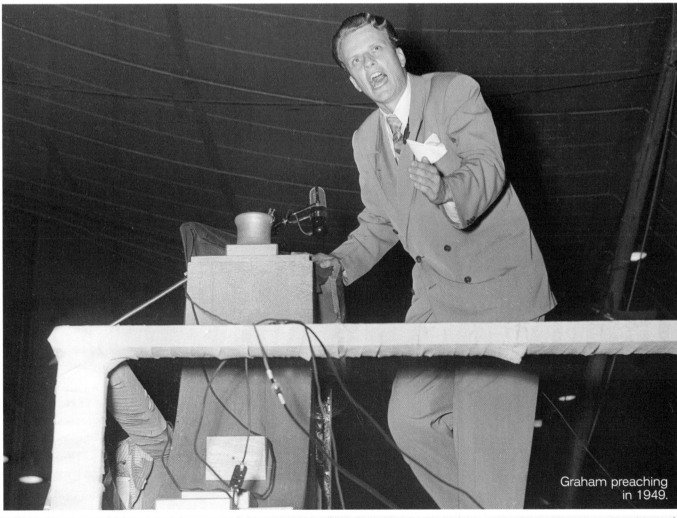

Graham preaching in 1949.

1950s.

outside and spit tobacco juice ("Wonder why he didn't just spit into the stove?" Graham would ask himself years later.) The most famous Graham song leader of all, Cliff Barrows, never had to excuse himself from directing the choir to go and spit!

Graham remembered the 40 or so ranchers and cowboys and their wives who came to hear the young preacher-to-be.

He remembered taking the pulpit in Bostwick with weak knees and a sweaty forehead. This infant of a preacher wound up using all four of the sermons he had prepared for four different nights. Added up, it only took him eight minutes to deliver the four messages. But it was eight minutes on one night in rural Florida that helped convince him this is what he had been called to do.

The Billy Graham Museum at Wheaton College in Illinois.

He moved on to Wheaton College in Illinois in September 1940, about 25 miles west of downtown Chicago. Early on, he was recruited by the Student Christian Council to preach at churches and

Ruth and Billy Graham in 1945.

Billy Graham's 40th birthday.

"When I came back from our first date," Ruth Graham recalled, "I remember telling the Lord, 'If you let me spend my life with that man, it would be the greatest privilege I could think of.'"

missions on weekends, not because of some high-minded spiritual reason — Graham was one of the few students on campus with a car.

After his first year, he returned home for the summer and was invited to preach a series of meetings in Charlotte on the wooded cam-

pus of Sharon Presbyterian Church, not far from his family's dairy farm. More than 60 years later, some of the fine, old men and women of Sharon still point to those meetings with deep pride and nostalgia. Our family has belonged to Sharon for years, and I'm often stopped by longtime members wanting to share a fact or remembrance of the day Billy Graham came to preach. I'm always glad to pause, and listen and proudly reminisce with them.

Wheaton College, Graham often said, was a spiritual and intellectual turning point in his life.

Billy and Ruth Graham in 1958.

The Graham family in 1957.

He recalled arriving at the college with his out-of-style clothes and Lil' Abner look about him, worried whether a Southern boy would fit in up north. He majored in anthropology because he thought it might come in handy if he entered the mission field. And he never forgot Dec. 7, 1941 — Pearl Harbor — and deciding after the attack that he needed to volunteer for the Army. Our armed forces were probably better off without him; he nearly killed a fellow student with his bayonet during a cadet training program on campus.

Graham remained in school after the war broke out, but the crisis gave him a deeper purpose and a new seriousness.

Wheaton also gave him something far more significant than a bachelor of arts degree in religion.

Billy and Ruth Bell Graham first met outside Williston Hall, the girls' dorm, in 1941. Billy was with a friend, Johnny Streater, and the two were in their sweaty work clothes because they had a little moving business going on the side and had been hauling furniture. But as soon as Johnny said, "Billy, here's the girl I was telling you about," the light went on.

It never went off, shining for all of Ruth Graham's 87 years. She passed away on June 14, 2007.

Billy described her as a slender, hazel-eyed movie starlet. In truth, Ruth McCue Bell was the daughter of Presbyterian medical missionaries Nelson and Virginia Bell, whose commitment to serving others led the family to the other side of the world. Ruth was born on Jun. 10, 1920, in China, where she spent her first 17 years living simply in the small town of Huaiyin. A one-smokestack town, she called it, looking back on her childhood with deep affection. Years later, she would reminisce about grow-

A poem the bride had written early in their life together captured the love that lasted for all their time together as partners: "I'd dreamt of shoulders broad and straight, one built to lead; I met you once and knew that you were all I need."

ing up speaking English and Chinese, bathing weekly in an old tin tub and watching her parents care for others.

On the first date at Wheaton with the man who would change her life, Billy took Ruth to a Sunday afternoon production of Handel's "Messiah." They were hooked, instantly.

"When I came back from our first date," Ruth Graham recalled, "I remember telling the Lord, 'If you let me spend my life with that man, it would be the greatest privilege I could think of.'"

In July of 1941, she accepted his proposal of marriage, inspiring the groom-to-be to stay up late into the night reading and rereading the letter in which she had said "Yes!" to him.

The first time they kissed on the lips is when he gave her the engagement ring back home in western North Carolina.

On Aug. 13, 1943, they were married at Montreat Presbyterian Church, in the mountain town where Ruth's parents and so many other Presbyterian missionaries have gone to retire over the years. A poem the bride had written early in their life together captured the love that lasted for all their time together as partners: "I'd dreamt of shoulders broad and straight, one built to lead; I met you once and knew that you were all I need."

Before it led to the Forest Home retreat center in California and the decision he made there, the long road first took the newly married husband to all corners of the globe.

Graham began his worldwide ministry with Youth for Christ, a Chicago-based ministry that gave

Ruth and Billy Graham in 1963.

him his first chance to show off the electric style that was soon to rivet all eyes on him.

It was what one writer called "a new kind of revival," one in which Graham took the pulpit with a Bible in one hand, a newspaper in the other and a powerful urge to tell people to get straight or else. It also foreshadowed the crusades to come, when Graham would pull his illustrations from current events to dramatize the age-old lessons of the Bible.

Whether he traveled by plane, train or Greyhound bus, through the United States or Europe, it didn't matter. Everywhere he went through the 1940s, Graham exuded the confidence — cockiness even — of a preacher sure of his message.

The young married couple traveled together at first — until they had the first of their five children, and Ruth was called to serve more as mother and homemaker in Montreat than companion to a preacher on the fly.

Ruth would try to hide how hard this lifestyle was behind jokes that became a familiar part of her public person. She was going to write a book, she said, and the working title would be, "How to Marry a Preacher and Remain a Christian." She never thought about divorce, she'd say to reporters wanting to know what it was like having a husband and father away for months at a time. But she did think a time or two about murder.

The truth?

The truth was that it was hard and sad for husband, wife and all the children to be constantly apart.

That fact was revealed in a lovely book about her life — *Footprints of a Pilgrim: The Life and Loves of Ruth Bell Graham.* There she reminisces about sleeping with her husband's tweed jacket the many nights they each spent alone. It was all she had of a husband she knew she must share with the

KANSAS CITY STAR FILE PHOTO

CHARLOTTE OBSERVER FILE PHOTO

The Graham family. The children are (L to R) Nelson, 4 days; Franklin, 5; Ruth, 7; Virginia, 12; and Anne, 9.

world.

The trip to California with Templeton was the one trip above all the others that changed everything.

By the time Graham and fellow Youth for Christ evangelist Charles Templeton arrived out west, they had been dubbed The Gold Dust Twins. It didn't matter where their ministry took them — Chicago, Charlotte, Toronto, Detroit, London. The two young preachers in the flashy ties were able to stir the masses.

And yet, early on, Templeton began to see that his friend was able to get a few more people to answer the altar call at the ends of each service — that pivotal moment in an evangelical Christian gathering where the preacher exhorts the people to come forward and surrender their lives to Christ.

While Graham was digging into his ministry, Templeton was begin-

Charles Templeton and Graham talked and debated off and on for a year — about the Bible and whether it is God's literal, perfect word or simply a fascinating account of the times.

ning to back away, beginning to doubt the worth of wooing people's hearts and not their minds, beginning to wonder whether it was right to stress emotion and ignore intellect.

The Gold Dust Twins began to pull apart. Templeton had been accepted to Princeton Theological Seminary and pleaded with Graham to join him at the fortress of scholarship. Graham said he couldn't go because he had made a commitment in 1947 to become president of Northwestern Schools in Minnesota. (Ever wonder why the Billy Graham Evangelistic Association wound up in a nondescript office building in downtown Minneapolis before moving to Charlotte? There's your answer.)

The two talked and debated off and on for a year — about the Bible and whether it is God's literal, perfect word or simply a fascinating account of the times. Templeton challenged Graham's whole premise upon which his young ministry was based, arguing that it is wrong not to think all the way through these things.

By the time they reached California and the conference of young, curious and questioning Christians, the rift was wide.

"I challenged him intellectually," Templeton told Graham's hometown newspaper, *The Charlotte Observer.* "The idea that there is a God of love in a world where horror and pain and suffering is so great. The idea that the Bible is the word and will of God, literally."

Graham felt the sting of being pushed to the wall by Templeton: "He felt I had gone too far in believing the Bible," Graham told

The Observer. "Taking it like I do. Following it. It bothered me. They were just challenging my strong faith in my belief in God."

At just 30 years of age, the young evangelist faced a crossroads. With an important crusade looming in Los Angeles — more important than he ever could have known — Graham knew he would have to give up evangelizing if he couldn't believe what he was imploring others to believe.

Graham recalled in his 1997 autobiography what happened next:

"I got up and took a walk. The moon was out. The shadows were long in the San Bernardino Mountains surrounding the retreat center. Dropping to my knees there in the woods, I opened the Bible at random on a tree stump in front of me. I could not read it in the shadowy moonlight, so I had no idea what text lay before me. Back at Florida Bible Institute, that kind of woodsy setting had given me a natural pulpit for proclamation. Now it was an altar where I could only stutter into prayer.

"The exact wording of my prayer is beyond recall, but it must have echoed my thoughts: 'O God! There are many things in this book I do not understand. There are many problems with it for which I have no solution. There are many seeming contradictions. There are some areas in it that do not seem to correlate with modern science. I can't answer some of the philosophical and psychological questions Chuck (Templeton) and others are raising.'

"I was trying to be on the level with God, but something remained unspoken. At last the Holy Spirit freed me to say it, 'Father, I am

William Randolph Hearst.

going to accept this as Thy Word — by faith! I'm going to allow faith to go beyond my intellectual questions and doubts, and I will believe this to be Your inspired Word.'

"When I got up from my knees at Forest Home that August night, my eyes stung with tears. I sensed the presence and power of God as I had not sensed it in months. Not all my questions were answered, but a major bridge had been crossed. In my heart and mind, I knew a spiritual battle in my soul had been fought and won."

It was done.

That night by the rock in the woods signaled a break in the union that had been forged by Graham and Templeton.

Templeton left the ministry in 1954 and eventually returned to his hometown of Toronto, where he wrote books and hosted a radio show. Though the two remained friends, Templeton believes that that night in the woods led Graham into what he called a life of "cosmic loneliness."

"He deliberately, as an act of will, decided not to think outside certain

"Puff Graham."

parameters," Templeton told *The Charlotte Observer* nearly five decades later. "He closed his eyes to these things. I feel that Billy cheated himself out of part of life — I think that when anyone closes his mind, he is denying a significant part of his life. That's a very dreadful step to take — A very sad day."

After an extraordinary, colorful life laced with both faith and doubt, Charles Templeton died on Jun. 7, 2001, following a long struggle with Alzheimer's disease. He was 85. The last years of his life were spent far from the public eye.

And Billy Graham?

Within a couple of months of that evening by the rock, he headed to Los Angeles, where he led a crusade that was to change his life.

It wasn't the crusade, actually, that changed his life as much as it was two words that affected the lives of millions of Christians the world over:

"Puff Graham."

Billy Graham's 1996 crusade in Charlotte, N.C.

THE GREAT CRUSADER

A Billy Graham crusade. The phrase rings with a thousand unforgettable images, doesn't it?

A football stadium set against a city's sleek skyline, packed with thousands of believers who have come on this night not to cheer on athletes but to praise God.

A massive stage filled with preachers, civic leaders, famous hometown athletes, singers, celebrities and one striking man in a business suit who stands at the center of attention.

An evening of music and messages, capped by a sermon setting forth the Gospel in terms any believer can understand and any skeptic can easily embrace.

And then an altar call unlike any other, when thousands rise from the seats and bleachers and pour onto the field.

This is exactly when a Billy Graham crusade reaches its peak, when it becomes as powerful a part of the Christian culture as a Sunday morning hymn at a Main Street church:

A mass choir made up of thousands of your friends and neighbors gently sings "Just As I Am." They'll be telling their grandkids about this for years to come.

The silver-haired evangelist comforts the thousands coming forward, telling them not to worry, we'll wait for you, just keep on coming and coming.

In great waves — some smiling, some dabbing at tears, some wrapping their arms around their children — they arrive at the foot of the stage and are met by volunteers handing out pamphlets, smiles and hugs.

From the top of the stadium, you can barely make out the evangelist whose authority lifted these people

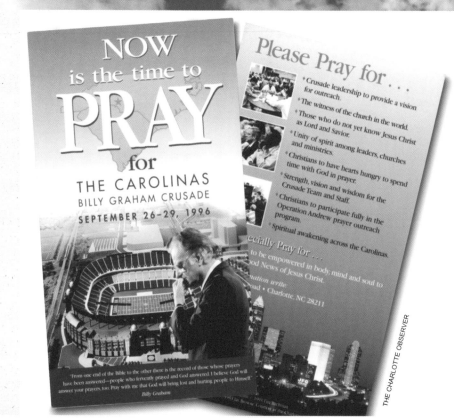

NOW is the time to PRAY for THE CAROLINAS
BILLY GRAHAM CRUSADE
SEPTEMBER 26-29, 1996

"From one end of the Bible to the other there is the record of those whose prayers have been answered—people who fervently prayed and God answered. I believe God will answer your prayers, too. Pray with me that God will bring lost and hurting people to Himself."
Billy Graham

Please Pray for . . .

• Crusade leadership to provide a vision for outreach.
• The witness of the church in the world.
• Those who do not yet know Jesus Christ as Lord and Savior.
• Unity of spirit among leaders, churches and ministries.
• Christians to have hearts hungry to spend time with God in prayer.
• Strength, vision and wisdom for the Crusade Team and Staff.
• Christians to participate fully in the Operation Andrew prayer outreach program.
• Spiritual awakening across the Carolinas.

Especially Pray for . . .
. . . to be empowered in body, mind and soul to . . . Good News of Jesus Christ.
. . . mation write
. . . Road • Charlotte, NC 28211

Michael W. Smith performing at Billy Graham's 1996 crusade in Charlotte, N.C.

The Gaither Vocal Band.

out of their seats. But you can see all the people who answered his call to commit their lives to Christ — maybe for the first time, maybe for the hundredth time in hopes this will be the one that sticks.

Together, they have come together — the evangelist and his people — in a moment that defines them all: A Billy Graham crusade.

The images tell you almost everything you need to know to understand the man and the mark he has left in modern Christianity.

There are a thousand reasons why we know Graham — from his books, *Decision* magazine, radio show, ministry movies; from his life spent beside kings and presidents; from his ascent to the top of every Most-Admired-Man-in-America list through much of the last half of the

Franklin Graham discussing Operation Christmas Child with former *Charlotte Observer* religion editor Ken Garfield.

Franklin Graham addressing volunteers at Operation Christmas Child.

20th Century; from these last years spent quietly at home, looking back.

But the main reason we know Graham, and the main reason so many of his followers learned to know Christ, is from his crusades, which ended in 2005.

They defined his ministry, they reflected who he was and what he believed, they gave him his primary stage, they captured the media's attention, and they will never be equaled in our lifetime.

Supporters and critics wonder all the time whether someone will come along to pack stadiums by the power of their compelling persona and fiery message.

Will it be Billy's son, Franklin, who now runs his father's ministry?

Anne Graham Lotz preaching in 1999.

JEFF SINER/THE CHARLOTTE OBSERVER

Greg Laurie in 1996.

BOB LEVERONE/THE CHARLOTTE OBSERVER

Or his daughter, Anne Graham Lotz, whose ministry to women grows more powerful with each arena gathering? Or California evangelist Greg Laurie, a Graham associate whose gift is for reaching the young and unchurched (which explains why he quotes Madonna, loves The Beatles and rides a Harley motorcycle). I can personally attest to another one of Laurie's gifts — his sense of humor. After writing a profile in which I said he looked like professional wrestler Hulk Hogan, Laurie sent me a T-shirt picturing his balding head on top of Hogan's muscular physique.

Or will the next Billy Graham be Argentina-born Luis Palau or some other evangelist who has tapped into the fervor of the international evangelical Christian world?

The answer always comes back the same.

These men and women might fill hotel ballrooms and the occasional indoor arena — but probably not stadiums. They are known to many — but not nearly to all. And none will likely ever possess the near-universal popularity, power or savvy to do what Billy Graham did:

To come along at a time when Christians in America and the world needed someone to latch onto. And to be the person who could accept that responsibility and not abuse it.

27

Luis Palau preaching in 1997.

Supporters and critics wonder all the time whether someone will come along to pack stadiums by the power of their compelling persona and fiery message.

It's the miracle of who Billy Graham is. And it all goes back to two words a publisher in Los Angeles uttered in 1949.

Graham had come to Los Angeles just weeks after his revelation in the San Bernardino Mountains, invited to share the Gospel by a group of businessmen who called themselves Christ for Greater Los Angeles.

He was to preach under a tent for three weeks starting in late September 1949. Graham, already partners by this point with gospel singer George Beverly Shea and music director Cliff Barrows, asked the committee to broaden church support for the campaign, and to put up a bigger tent. Even early on, they were savvy marketers of the ministry.

The part about the bigger tent was more wishful thinking than prophecy; this was to be an important crusade in the young and growing career of the evangelist, but nothing anyone thought would shake the earth under his feet.

The Los Angeles crusade opened with 3,000 or so coming to hear Graham on weeknights, perhaps 4,000 on the bigger Sundays. There were empty seats at the start, and yet Graham sensed he was preaching with newfound fervor after deciding that summer in the mountains never to doubt God and the Bible.

"There was no gap between what I said and what I knew I believed deep in my soul," he wrote in his autobiography. "It was

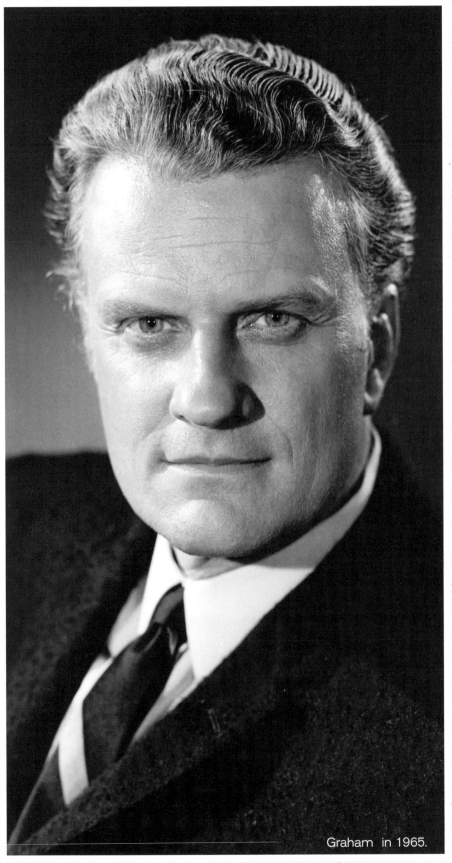

Graham in 1965.

no coincidence that the centerpiece of the 150-foot platform in the tent, right in front of the pulpit, was a replica of an open Bible — twenty feet high, and twenty feet wide."

With the crowds beginning to grow in number and intensity, in part due to support from some Hollywood celebrities of the time like Colleen Townsend and Stuart Hamblen, Graham decided to extend the crusade beyond its

> *The main reason we know Billy Graham, and the main reason so many of his followers learned to know Christ, is from his crusades.*

three-week run. But he had no clue what was to come, until he arrived at the tent one October night and was met by a crowd of L.A. reporters and photographers normally drawn only to politicians, movie stars and scandals.

When he asked one of the reporters, who had been a no-show at the crusade until this night, what was going on, he got the answer that changed everything.

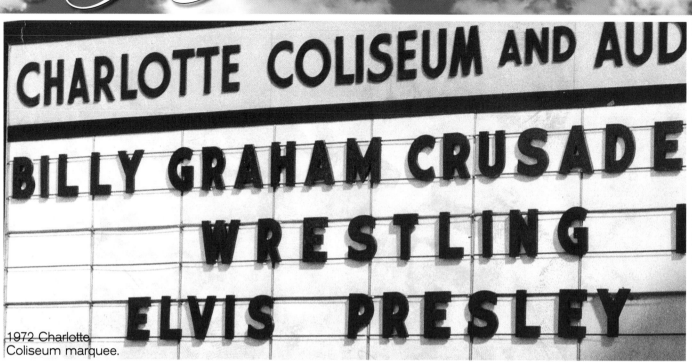

CHARLOTTE COLISEUM AND AUD

BILLY GRAHAM CRUSADE

WRESTLING

ELVIS PRESLEY

1972 Charlotte
Coliseum marquee.

(From left) Roy Rogers, Dale Evans,
Billy Graham, June Carter Cash and
Johnny Cash.

Graham estimated that 82 percent of the thousands of people who committed their lives to Christ during his Los Angeles crusade had been unchurched to that point.

"You've just been kissed by William Randolph Hearst," the reporter told him.

Hearst was the powerful, almost mythical newspaper publisher who owned the *Los Angeles Examiner*, the *Los Angeles Herald Express* and other newspapers in great cities across the nation. Today, many know him as the inspiration for the dark, complex, central character in the 1941 Orson Welles film classic, *Citizen Kane*.

But back then, he was a man who could shape the public culture with one command, and in Graham he saw something extraordinary.

Graham and Hearst had never so much as corresponded or spoken in person or by phone before one changed the other's life. For the rest of his years, Graham wasn't exactly sure whether the newspaper king was inspired by the N.C. native's Christian faith or the way he could magnetize a crowd. Hearst might simply have seen in Graham's tent crusade a way to sell some more papers. After World War II, on the edge of the Cold War, historians say Hearst might have been impressed by the patriotism reflected in Graham's early sermons.

Whatever the reason, what Hearst did in the fall of 1949 in Los Angeles moved mountains and moved them swiftly.

"Puff Graham," Hearst was said to have ordered his editors, meaning for them to pull out all stops on publicity.

Suddenly, Hearst papers — with the competition quickly keeping pace — began running front-page stories and photos of this lanky Southern preacher. The publicity helped fill the tent with followers drawn by word of his magnetism.

He was being compared to Billy Sunday, until then America's most famous Christian evangelist.

The crowds swelled; 3,000 more chairs were added as the crusade entered its fifth week.

A Los Angeles County judge, Graham recalled, sentenced some convicted criminals to go and get some religion.

On Nov. 20, 1949, a Sunday afternoon more than a month after the original closing date, 11,000 packed the tent for the last of

Billy Graham in 1996.

CHRISTOPHER A. RECORD/THE CHARLOTTE OBSERVER

Billy Graham and music director Cliff Barrows in 1996.

Graham's 72 meetings. Thousands more were forced to try to hear from outside.

He had preached 65 full sermons, led 72 meetings attended by 350,000 over eight weeks, given dozens of interviews, and been the subject of who knows how many positive stories in newspapers, magazines and on TV and radio. Ever the records-keeper, a hallmark of his precise organization, Graham estimated that 82 percent of the thousands of people who committed their lives to Christ during his Los Angeles crusade had been unchurched to that point.

The cynical might say this was all because an eccentric media magnate decided to hype Graham.

The faithful say it's because God's hand was behind this historic connection between two men. Ruth Graham told her husband that God might have used Hearst to promote the meetings, "but the credit belonged solely to God."

Historians say the time was ripe for a charismatic evangelist with a simple, optimistic message to captivate America. World War II had just ended, the men who survived had returned from battle and begun

to put down roots and start families. Church attendance hit its peak in America at around that time. Religious historian Sidney Ahlstrom called this revival of religious activity in the late 1940s and early 1950s "a surge of piety."

People were searching for meaning, stability and peace after the terrible war. They found it in their neighborhood church. And they found it in an evangelist who had the foresight in 1949 to realize that life after Los Angeles would never be the same.

"All I knew was that before it was over," Graham wrote, "we were on a journey from which there would be no looking back."

There was no stopping Graham now.

He began his foray into films in connection with a 1950 crusade in Portland, Ore., eventually reaching more than 100 million people through that medium. His World Wide Pictures has produced more than 125 films since the 1953 *Souls in Conflict*, always insisting that the Christian message be articulated with Hollywood-style quality. One of his films, *The Climb*, was even shown in multiplex theaters around the country in 2002.

He founded his *Hour of Decision* radio program, carried over the years by hundreds of stations.

He established the non-profit Billy Graham Evangelistic Association in Minneapolis, filling leadership positions with the men who would stay at his side for a lifetime — Barrows, Shea, and brothers Grady and T.W. Wilson.

Barrows and Shea, who passed away in 2013, in particular, became two-thirds of modern Christianity's greatest trio.

> *"All I knew was that before it was over, we were on a journey from which there would be no looking back." There was no stopping Graham now.*

Barrows was the cheerful master of ceremonies at the crusades, directing the choir and keeping the program moving. While he dreamed as a child of being a doctor, he found his calling at a Baptist youth conference in Tennessee in the 1940s. When Graham suddenly needed a fill-in pianist and singer, he recruited Cliff and Billie Barrows from the audience. "It wasn't too big a beginning," Cliff Barrows said. "But it was good enough."

The Canadian-born Shea pro-

George Beverly Shea in 1997. He died in 2013.

DIEDRA LAIRD/THE CHARLOTTE OBSERVER

33

No city, though, matched the lasting impact and electricity of New York City. Over 16 weeks in the spring and summer of 1957, Graham preached to more than two million people.

vided the sound of the crusade. He had a deep, booming voice, and had been singing for the Lord long before Graham first welcomed him to a stage in 1943 to share what became their signature hymn, "How Great Thou Art."

"A long time ago," Barrows once said, "God gave us (Shea and me) both a tremendous gift. He gave us the desire to work with Bill, to help him touch people. It's a gift neither of us could ever pay back."

Soon after Los Angeles, Graham began making a name for himself in Europe, preaching to thousands in London in 1954 and meet-

ing with Prime Minister Winston Churchill — a foreshadowing of his close associations to come with U.S. presidents.

Then came the crusade that cemented the fame that had begun to blossom in Los Angeles.

Graham would eventually preach to more than 210 million people in 185 countries and territories before his crusades ended. Perhaps the most striking handout from his ministry is the four-page, alphabetized list of cities where he preached. It begins with Aarhus, Denmark, in 1955, and ends with Zurich, Switzerland, in 1955 and

Billy Graham in Central Park in 1991.

Graham in New York, 1954.

1960. In between are hundreds of cities large and small, where millions, young and old, had their eyes opened and their hearts touched.

No city, though, matched the lasting impact and electricity of New York City. Over 16 weeks in the spring and summer of 1957, Graham preached to more than 2 million people in venues we all know — Madison Square Garden, Yankee Stadium and, finally, a Sept. 1 rally that packed Times Square.

This being New York, a city that savors passionate debate, not every-

one welcomed Graham. Some liberals found him too simple. Some conservatives found him too ecumenical. Some Jews and Catholics thought he was coming to convert them.

But Graham won most of the critics over, preaching night after night on the hope found in faith. Even on 42nd Street. "Here in Times Square," he preached, "is the dope addict, the alcoholic, the harlot. Tonight for a few moments it is being turned into a great cathedral."

Years later, he recalls the details of the crusade that solidified what

had first begun to take root in Los Angeles:

The 100,000 who packed Yankee Stadium on a 90-degree day, with another 20,000 standing outside. The 60,000 who came forward to say yes to Christ. The 99 times that Bev Shea figured he sang "How Great Thou Art." The night a priest and a prostitute answered the altar call. The night then-Vice President Richard Nixon came — the beginning of Graham's association with politicians. The night he appeared on *The Steve Allen Show* on TV with

Hollywood's Pearl Bailey, Dean Jones and Tallulah Bankhead — the beginning of his foray into secular areas foreign to most religious figures of his day.

There was comfort in walking into a stadium and knowing you were going to receive testimonials from VIPs, music from celebrities, a sermon from Graham and then an altar call to end all altar calls. A Billy Graham crusade spanned our world for parts of two centuries.

Graham left New York exhausted from the 16 weeks of preaching, but emboldened by the acclaim he earned in a city that stands at the center of the world.

And yet, what happened in New York happened most everywhere Graham went. While the culture and crowds in each city differed, there was a trademark quality to a crusade that crossed continents and eras.

Whether it was Copenhagen, Denmark, in 1954, Charlotte, N.C., in 1996 or Dallas, Tex., in 2002, the preparation and execution of each event was strikingly similar.

It was part of the ministry's gift for promotion and public relations, putting on the same event in the same way and drawing huge crowds everywhere they went.

But it was more than that: It was Graham offering the comfort that came from Christians knowing what they are going to get at one of his crusades. Just as there is comfort in opening your Bible to a familiar passage, there was comfort in walking into a stadium and knowing you were going to receive testimonials from VIPs, music from celebrities, a sermon from Graham and then an altar call to end all altar calls.

And there was comfort knowing this went on year after year, era after

Using a program to shield herself from the afternoon heat a woman bows her head in prayer at the Greater New York Billy Graham Crusade at Flushing Meadows Corona Park Sunday, June 26, 2005.

brand-new Ericsson Stadium, Scott Lenning moved in to help run the crusade operation.

"Moved" was the operative word, because Lenning's life was spent moving from one crusade to the next, helping plan the event and then moving to the next town for the next undertaking. His wife, Tami, and their children appreciated the journey that took them to more than a dozen cities — they put a personalized license plate on the family vehicle that said "MOVNAGN."

Why make such a sacrifice for Billy Graham?

"To see the impact of his crusades on people's lives," Lenning told me years ago. "To know you had a part in it."

The months leading up to each crusade would be filled with public prayer meetings, stories in the local press, paid advertising, bumper stickers and billboards, all aimed at whipping up interest. Knowing what Hearst did for him in 1949, no religious figure courted the secular press more masterfully than Graham.

Yet another example of Graham's media savvy came in early 2003. Promoting a San Diego crusade scheduled for May 8-11, his association reported that more than 20,000 people attended training sessions to serve as volunteers at the meetings — double the number anticipated and matched by only three other past crusades. A small fact, probably of interest to few outside the ministry. But enough to generate one more headline.

When he was younger and more fit, he'd host dozens of reporters weeks before his crusade,

era. Times changed. Styles lived and died. Generations passed.

But a Billy Graham crusade spanned our world for parts of two centuries.

Plans for one of these crusades grew like clockwork:

Graham would only put on a crusade in a city whose civic, political and religious leaders first came together to invite him. He had an idea where his ministry needed to go; but first he'd wait for a groundswell of support he

helped to plant, and an invitation he helped arrange.

Then the legendary Graham advance planning would set in.

A local committee made up of secular movers and spiritual shakers would be formed to organize and promote the crusade, working with a team of Graham staffers who would travel from city to city planning these crusades. In his hometown of Charlotte in 1996, where his crusade was one of the first nonfootball events at then

Johnny Cash and Billy Graham in 1996.

an interview sure to generate front-page publicity. Before his 1996 crusade in Charlotte, the Grahams welcomed 100 journalists to their home in Montreat. After the front-porch interviews and TV shots for the overeager TV anchors, the Grahams welcomed a *Charlotte Observer* colleague and myself for a private lunch. Over McDonald's burgers and ice cream, we chatted informally about this and that.

Graham had us beaming with stories about the day Muhammad Ali came to lunch in 1979, and accepted an autographed Bible from the evangelist that said "God Bless You" and then Graham's name, both

Billy and Ruth Graham with Muhammad Ali.

Graham in 1996.

Billy Graham hugging
Michael Tait of dc Talk.

in a hard-to-read scrawl.

Ali handed it back to Graham and said, "How about printing 'Billy Graham' under that. I want people to know it's you when I show it to them."

It was a memorable afternoon for me, one I shared later with readers in a story before the crusade. It was a win-win situation — we all got to see the Grahams with their guard down.

Then, a few days before the start of the crusade, he'd arrive in town for another news conference, pose for a photo op riding around the stadium on a golf cart and then perhaps spend a few moments granting a one-on-one interview with the major hometown daily newspaper.

Given his fame and integrity, Graham probably could have packed stadiums without the buzz he helped generate. But it didn't hurt to get on the front page, above the fold, or to inspire special newspaper sections promoting the coming of the crusade.

39

Jeannie Danielson of Charlotte, N.C. raises her hands in prayer during the 1996 Charlotte crusade.

By the time the crusade arrived, it was the talk of the town, capturing the imagination of Christians focused on the message as well as others focused on the sheer spectacle of it all.

The crusade itself was as carefully staged as the promotion leading up to it. What unfolded in Charlotte in September 1996 before 305,000 people over four nights echoed the experience that millions of others have had worldwide.

Each night, the stadium opened at 6 p.m. for the thousands who came with their children in the family minivan or their Sunday school class in the church bus. A local dignitary or athlete would say a few words, then a well-known performer would share his faith in song. In Charlotte, a weathered Johnny Cash gave his gravely voice to the classic "Precious Memories," with his wife, June, providing the perfect harmony.

On the Saturday night of each crusade, Youth Night drew a packed stadium for Christian rock music and a youth-oriented sermon from Graham. In Charlotte, the interracial trio dc Talk and soloist Michael W. Smith performed, and Graham's message included a reference to "Bullet With Butterfly Wings," a hit song of the time by the rock group Smashing Pumpkins.

Graham's last crusade visit to his hometown ended on a perfect autumn Sunday night in September. The Gaither Vocal Band wrapped its four-part harmony around "Because He Lives." Graham turned around and offered a wave of thanks to the choir. The altar call drew thousands. And it was over.

But it wasn't over before Graham offered four sermons, each with a different illustration and focus — but each with the same finishing theme. This is why the crusades drew millions over decades, and why each sermon began with a gentle order to open the book you brought with you.

"I hope that you will bring your Bibles every night," he preached at the start, "because I would like to talk from the Bible, and tell you what the Bible says. You know, we hear the voices of all the political

Billy Graham's image was projected on a large video board at a crusade in Kansas City in 2004.

people and all of the psychiatrists, the psychologists, the sociologists, everybody. The time has come for us to listen to the voice of God, and to see what God has to say, and if we did that and obeyed God, our problems could be solved overnight...."

Thursday in Charlotte, I sat with thousands as he spoke of the brevity of life, and the need to recognize that we are all born with sin and there is only one cure for the disease.

Jesus is the cure, he said. Jesus is the fixed star in the sky on whom we need to keep our eyes.

Friday he focused on the value of each of our souls. "There's an eternal destiny for every soul," he said, "and

Rolando Pina, 15, left, and Jazmin Bernal, 15, right, adjusted their AM radio transmitters to listen to the simulcast in Spanish of the Billy Graham Crusade.

it's determined by a choice that you make here in this life...."

On a rainy Saturday night, he talked to the 88,000 youth who had packed the stadium and spilled outside about gangs, teen suicide and drugs. He challenged them to quit worrying about being most popular and start thinking instead about accepting Christ.

"What is a Christian?" he asked. "I believe a Christian is three things. He's a person that's made a choice. He's a person that's accepted a challenge. And he's a person that's been changed."

Sunday, in his final sermon in the city where he was born, Graham urged the crowd to be ready when Judgment Day comes.

"This is the last service," he preached. "We probably will never see anything like this again in the history of Charlotte. Look at me. You have a moment before God that may never come again. I'm going to ask you to come. And say yes to Christ. You don't understand it all, or have to. You just say, 'Lord, I'm willing to surrender my life to you. I want you to come in and be the Lord and master of my life....'"

As it all came to an end, Charlotte poet and columnist Dannye Romine Powell wrote: "Cameras flash. Binoculars rise. People linger in the aisles and at the railings for one final look. The simple man with the simple message. Of this place and of this soil. Charlotte will not soon forget."

Over four nights, I heard Graham preach his messages and plead with the huge crowd to respond. Then I stood on the stadium floor, dodging people answering the altar call, watching them shed tears, smile wide and turn their lives over to God because this evangelist asked them to.

I can still see their faces, still recall their stories. I won't forget any of them.

There was Alma Keener and her pal, Anna Martin, a couple of Amish Mennonites in their 70s who rode all day by bus for this privilege. They giggled so hard their prayer shawls nearly fell off their heads.

There was Jo Ann Key, confined to a wheelchair by post-polio syndrome but still able to bounce to the chorus of "Jesus Came into My Heart."

Graham preached much of his career about racial reconciliation, how we are all brothers and sisters no matter our color or culture. Here was the sermon come to life, before my eyes. As she moved to the music, Key, who is white, leaned over the stadium rail to shake the

Billy and Franklin Graham in Charlotte, N.C. in 1996.

JOHN D. SIMMONS/THE CHARLOTTE OBSERVER

Spectators view Dr. Graham in Philadelphia, June 24, 1992.

THE PHILADELPHIA INQUIRER FILE PHOTO

hand of Erica Williams, a black woman she did not know until now.

Now, though, they were sisters in faith who exchanged "God bless yous."

There was 6-year-old John Hagan, heading to the children's service one bright Saturday morning on leg braces, huffing and puffing and announcing, "I pick up a little speed." Whenever I think about John, I think about *The Little Engine That Could*. And I smile.

There was Nellie Roth, watching thousands answer the altar call, recalling the Billy Graham rally 44 years earlier when her own mother answered the call and was saved. No wonder her green eyes glistened with tears.

I covered other crusades after that. I wrote about Graham getting the Congressional Gold Medal in the halls of Congress, and breaking ground for the Billy Graham

Evangelistic Association's move from Minneapolis to Charlotte. I watched him change the name of his events from crusades to missions because it sounded kinder and gentler.

I smiled as he teased us all at the Dallas crusade in Texas Stadium in 2002, hinting this might be the finale because of his fragile health. Within months, he had scheduled two more, vowing to go on until God called him home.

I saw the crowds get a bit smaller in some cities, and the Graham people have to market more aggressively. I noticed the emphasis shift to Youth Night and the Christian rock music sure to draw a full house. And as the years marched on, I could see Graham having to grip the podium ever tighter to keep his balance, his son and successor, Franklin, seated behind him, ready to get up and preach if his elderly father couldn't go on.

But he always went on.

On the final night in Charlotte, I found myself seated in a golf cart at the foot of the stage — the golf cart that would take Graham out of the stadium when it all was over. The altar call had ended, and here came the evangelist down the stairs and into the seat beside me. He looked tired and flushed, but I remember his eyes glistening so brightly.

We exchanged a few words, words that were hard to make out above the din of the crowd filing out and the rush of nervous aides all around us. But I knew then that this was a moment of faith not to be equaled in my life.

The long journey had taken Graham from Los Angeles to London to New York and most everyplace else, and now here he was beside me in Charlotte.

The Great Crusader at the close of another crusade. A moment in history, made by a man for all time.

43

AMERICA'S PREACHER

*I*t's the ultimate irony.

Billy Graham has devoted his life to the average people who came to his crusades, read his newspaper columns, magazines and books, watched his ministry's movies, fiddled with the radio to catch his *Hour of Decision* program each Sunday morning before church.

You could look up from the floor of a stadium into the vast crowd at any of his crusades over more than 50 years and see bankers sitting beside bricklayers, blacks beside whites, excited Pentecostals beside button-down Presbyterians. His were crusades for all Christians, led by an evangelist who didn't care who you were or what you did. He only cared about saving your soul, and all souls were equal.

And yet ...

And yet to many, Graham isn't just an evangelist for the people. He is a friend to the rich and famous, a man who could turn up in a Baptist church one day and on *The Tonight Show* with Johnny Carson the next.

On the good days, that meant he counseled celebrities and presidents, prayed with them, even led them to a deeper faith. The second President George Bush credited Graham with leading him away from a life of partying and alcohol, back to God, his family and his faith.

"We're told (in the Bible) to pray for the people in authority," Graham said years ago. "Jacob prayed for the Pharaoh and Daniel prayed for Nebuchadnezzar."

He was America's Preacher.
He embodied America's faith.

Billy Graham has devoted his life to the average people who came to his crusades, read his newspaper columns, magazines and books, watched his ministry's movies, fiddled with the radio to catch his Hour of Decision program each Sunday morning before church.

Billy Graham presented Pope John Paul II with a handmade quilt from the North Carolina mountains in 1990.

He was the one we turned to in times of need — as in 1995, when we needed to hear words of solace at the nationally televised memorial service after the Oklahoma City bombing. That was Graham there on stage with President Clinton, telling us that while he doesn't understand why this horrible tragedy happened, he understands this much: We can still turn to God in times of grief and anger. God will be there for us.

No one but Graham could have played the role of comforter and counselor so well for so long for so many people.

But on the darker days, Graham's brush with fame and glory took on a different hue. He was a man who allowed himself to become compro-

mised by the politics and power of which he chose to be a well-publicized part.

He admitted as much.

Later in his life, long after he distanced himself from all that, he confessed to having been seduced by the glare of acclaim, thus narrowing his reach to people of different political and religious persuasions. When you golfed with John F. Kennedy Jr. or prayed with Richard Nixon, it was easy to become blinded by the spotlight. And easy for some people to lose faith in you because of it.

Once, in 1964, he had to hold a news conference to squelch talk that he was considering running for the Republican presidential nomination.

No wonder his wife, Ruth, who

preceded him in death, once kicked her husband under the table when he went too far in partisan politics.

In a sense, it was another lesson Graham shared with the world, one learned the hard way:

Ultimately, it was best to be a simple preacher who tried to embrace everyone.

Graham's fascination with power grew from his N.C. upbringing. Raised on a dairy farm in Charlotte, far from the halls of fame and power, he became easily, understandably starry-eyed.

Simply put, he loved getting to know people who mattered, and that never changed. Couple that with his natural warmth, a disinclination to confront or challenge people and the evangelical belief that to change

Graham with President Ford.

someone you must first befriend them and you see why he reached out to everyone from Johnny Cash to both President Bushes. And why they always reached back to him as a friend and confidante.

"If I seem to concentrate on some of those friendships," Graham wrote in his autobiography, "it is only because I have come to know some of these leaders in a pastoral way and others simply as friends. Although people who are constantly in the public eye usually learn to shield their inner thoughts, they have the same personal problems and questions that we do. Sometimes such people feel free to talk intimately with me, knowing that I would hold their remarks in confidence."

Sit with him over a cup of coffee and talk would eventually turn to remembrances of golf games with Bob Hope (the legendary comic joked about finding Billy on his knees once in a sand trap, as if his prayers might help him shoot par);

Billy Graham with Kim Il Sung, president of North Korea.

TV appearances with Jack Benny, Jack Paar and Steve Allen; celebrity dinners at which he sat beside the likes of Zsa Zsa Gabor. The walls of his offices in Minneapolis, Charlotte and Montreat were lined with handsomely framed photos of the magazine covers on which he appeared and the TV shows on which he made small talk.

One poignant celebrity encounter came in 1996, when John F. Kennedy Jr. and his new bride, Carolyn, came to visit the Grahams in Montreat shortly after their much-publicized wedding. The couple was killed when their single-engine plane crashed into the Atlantic

Ocean in the summer of 1999. Graham recalled how he had sensed a growing spirituality in JFK Jr. the day they met for the last time, three years before the tragedy.

But it was Graham's connection to every U.S. president dating back to Harry Truman that remains the image ingrained in people's minds, and that cemented his reputation as Our Nation's Pastor.

That long, ultimately influential walk with our leaders didn't start out well, though.

It was the summer of 1950, Graham was on the fast track after his electrifying Los Angeles crusade and he and colleagues Grady Wilson, Cliff

Barrows and Jerry Beavan were off to Washington at the invitation of Harry Truman. The tough-talking Democrat from Missouri had issued the invitation after Graham wrote him a year earlier, promising the prayers of his students at Northwestern Schools in Minneapolis.

Having seen a newspaper photo of Truman wearing white buck shoes while on vacation in Florida, the quartet had what they thought at the time was a brainstorm — they'd all go out and get white buck shoes for their White House meeting! That would impress Truman, they figured.

It was all downhill from there. Graham recalled how Truman

Billy Graham with former Presidents Bush, Carter and Clinton in 2007.

must have thought he was meeting with a traveling vaudeville team. The N.C. evangelist spoke in support of Truman's get-tough policy against North Korea's invasion of South Korea — a sign of Graham's politically conservative streak to come. Then the overeager evangelist got down to the business of why he really wanted this meeting, peppering the President with questions about his faith, and whether he believed in Christ and His death on the cross.

Graham recalled Truman fudging his answer, saying he tries to live by the Golden Rule and Jesus' Sermon on the Mount, but that that was about it.

Not yet trained in the ways of diplomacy, Graham had the gall to tell Truman — to tell the most powerful man on earth — it wasn't enough, he needed to surrender all to Christ.

After 20 minutes, Truman had had enough of this. He stood up, signaling the end of the meeting.

Graham and Co. closed with a prayer, then stepped outside and were immediately pounced on by the aggressive press corps. Instead of heeding the tradition of honoring White House privacy, Graham recounted much of what went on inside for reporters and photographers, who were loving every naïve minute of this.

The capper came when Graham agreed to reenact their prayer with Truman — the preacher and his colleagues dropped to their knees on the White House lawn in their white bucks and pastel summer suits, making for a photo fit for every newspaper in the land.

Graham was never invited back to the Truman White House, not surprising considering what was said in a 1951 White House memo: "You remember what a show of himself Billy Graham made the last time he was here. The President does not want it repeated."

Years later, during a visit at Truman's home in Independence, Mo., the two men made up — older, wiser and more conciliatory about the past and each other.

From the rocky start with Truman, Graham learned the lessons of gentility and decorum. From Dwight D. Eisenhower on, he began to follow rather than lead when it came to our presidents; counsel rather than dictate; pray with rather than evangelize to.

Once, during a meeting he attended with President Nixon and some of his Republican allies in 1968

Billy Graham with President Truman.

to talk about a vice presidential running mate, a writer couldn't figure out exactly how to describe Graham.

So he listed him as "sidekick." Perfect!

He truly grew to become a sidekick to presidents, a man whose unique relationship with each one became part of his life story. And part of American lore.

It was Graham's connection to every U.S. president dating back to Harry Truman that remains the image ingrained in people's minds, and that cemented his reputation as Our Nation's Pastor.

DWIGHT D. EISENHOWER

There was none of the awkwardness between these two men that marked the relationship between Truman and Graham.

The war hero and the evangelist got along smoothly. Eisenhower used Graham as a sounding board to help deal with the racial unrest in America. Under Ike's administration, Graham and several other religious leaders started the Presidential Prayer Breakfast that grew to became the rich tradition now known as the National Prayer Breakfast. Fittingly, Billy Graham, and then his son, Franklin, preached many a sermon at that annual gathering of thousands in Washington.

Just as fittingly, Anne Graham Lotz carried on her father's tradition when she preached in April 1999 at the nation's second biggest prayer

Billy Graham with President Eisenhower.

AP WORLD WIDE PHOTOS

Billy Graham with President Kennedy.

Billy Graham welcomes Vice President and Mrs. Richard Nixon and their daughter Patricia to a Graham crusade at Washington's Griffith Stadium in 1960.

breakfast — the annual Easter gathering in Charlotte modeled after the Washington event. Before a sellout crowd of 1,900 at the new convention center uptown, Lotz echoed the evangelism of her father and brother when she all but begged the crowd: "Listen to me…. This Holy Week, you get right with God."

Just before Eisenhower died in 1969, the 34th President of the United States summoned Graham to his bedside at Walter Reed Army Hospital. He wanted some assurance that his sins were about to be forgiven and that he was destined for heaven.

Graham remembered pulling out his copy of the New Testament and reading from it as he held the President's hand gently in his.

Graham remembered what Eisenhower said then:

"Thank you. I'm ready."

JOHN F. KENNEDY

Graham didn't endorse a candidate in the bitterly fought race between Kennedy and Richard Nixon in 1960, though it was no secret Graham and Nixon were close friends. Graham admitted to making not-so-subtle references to his obvious preference for Nixon in a speech to the Southern Baptist Convention.

He nearly blew his neutrality, though, when he wrote a positive piece about Nixon for the wildly popular *Life* magazine. Graham wrote it, sent it, then had second thoughts about the wisdom of what he had just done. He fell to his knees in prayer with his wife, Ruth, asking God to halt its publication if that was His will. The next day, *Life* executive Henry Luce called to say he wasn't comfortable with the piece and pulled it. God, Graham felt, had intervened on his behalf.

Graham's association, good and bad, with Nixon is part of the evangelist's public legacy. But after Kennedy narrowly defeated Nixon to become the first Catholic to capture the White House, Graham became part of that president's legacy as well.

At Kennedy's invitation, Graham and the president-elect played a round of golf together in Palm Beach, Fla., just days before his inauguration in 1961. From Kennedy's perspective, it was a chance to gain the support of a Protestant religious leader and defuse the acrimony stirred by a Catholic about to assume the presidency. From Graham's perspective, it was a chance to gain another foothold in power.

Both sides gained, especially the President, when Graham told reporters that Kennedy should be judged on his ability and character and not on his religion.

The friendship, of course, didn't last long.

Graham said he had a foreboding before Nov. 22, 1963, that something terrible was about to happen. He was on the golf course in Black Mountain, N.C., near his Montreat home, when he got the news from Dallas.

He sat beside the Kennedy family at the funeral in Washington.

LYNDON B. JOHNSON

At the 1973 funeral for the Texas-born-and-bred president, Graham described LBJ as "a mountain of a man with a whirlwind for a heart."

Except for Nixon, Graham probably spent more time with his fellow Southerner than any other president. They talked, swam, prayed and flew together on various presidential trips.

On occasion, LBJ even asked Graham to cross the line from preaching into politics. During a White House dinner in 1964, LBJ reviewed a list of potential vice presidential running mates, then asked Graham which one he ought to go with.

The ever-feisty Ruth Graham intervened, saying her husband ought to limit his opinions to matters of faith, not politics.

A few moments, later, out of his wife's earshot, Graham told LBJ, "Hubert Humphrey."

LBJ — with Humphrey on the ticket — swamped Republican arch-conservative Barry Goldwater of Arizona in November.

> *Except for Nixon, Graham probably spent more time with his fellow Southerner than any other president. They talked, swam, prayed and flew together on various presidential trips.*

CHARLOTTE OBSERVER FILE PHOTO

Graham with President Lyndon B. Johnson.

RICHARD NIXON

They met around 1950 in Washington, long before Nixon rose to the presidency and then fell in disrepute over Watergate. Their friendship covered golf, family, faith and politics, and was powerful enough to shame Graham long after he eulogized Nixon at his funeral in 1994.

The two took to each other quickly — a Quaker from California and a Baptist from North Carolina intent on raising their profiles in their chosen professions.

Looking back after Watergate and the President's terrible language caught on tape, Graham wondered whether he had overemphasized Nixon's spirituality. But at the time, before the truth became known, there was nothing to come between them.

In late 1967, Nixon summoned Graham to Key Biscayne, Fla., where they attended church together, watched a Green Bay Packers football game on TV and took a long, important walk toward a lighthouse on the beach.

Somewhere during those two miles together in the sand, Nixon wanted to know what Graham thought of him running for President in 1968, eight years after he had narrowly lost to JFK.

"If you don't run," Graham recalled saying, "you will always wonder if you should have. I will pray for you, that the Lord will give you the wisdom to make the right choice."

The rest belongs to history.

Graham prayed at both Nixon inaugurations, in 1968 and 1972.

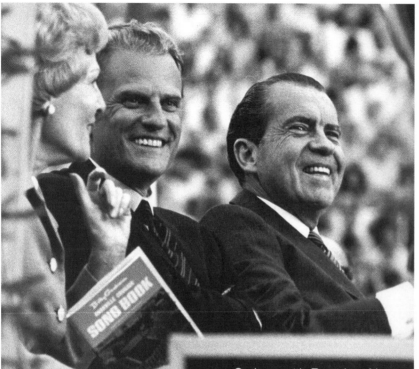

Graham with President Nixon.

When he heard Nixon's harsh language on the tape, Graham understood. He threw up, then wrote and spoke publicly about it, calling the sordid affair a symptom of a deeper moral crisis.

The shadow that Nixon cast over Graham didn't fade with the President's death. The release of tapes in 2002 revealed that Graham had made disparaging remarks about Jews in a conversation with Nixon in the Oval Office 30 years earlier. Despite saying he didn't recall the conversation, Graham apologized once, then apologized a second time, a sign of contrition accepted by many.

"His actions speak much

The President came to Charlotte in 1971 when Graham's hometown honored him with a "Billy Graham Day." Despite some hecklers protesting the Vietnam War, the two smiled like conquering heroes as they made their way through the downtown masses in a convertible, Nixon teaching Graham how to shake this many hands without hurting himself.

Then came Watergate in 1972, Nixon's resignation, the shaming of his presidency and the release of the White House tapes filled with Nixon's vulgarity.

Graham knew little about Watergate. He had doubted up until then that his friend could have done something so foolish, illegal and immoral as to sanction a break-in at a Democratic Party office and then try to cover it up.

From left, Kathie Lee Gifford, the Rev. Billy Graham and former President Gerald R. Ford in 1999.

Graham with former President Jimmy Carter.

would put the nation once more through the torment of Watergate.

Ford, of course, pardoned Nixon — a move that today seems one inspired more by mercy than partisanship.

One more piece of personal business between Graham and Ford involved Ruth Graham: on a visit to Charlotte to deliver a speech, Ford was greeted by a heckler who stood up and blocked the view of some in the audience. One angry audience member turned out to be Ruth Graham, who jerked the sign from the protester and wound up being sued for it.

After the case was dismissed, Ford called her to say, "Ruth, I think what you did was a very courageous thing."

JIMMY CARTER

One would have thought these two men would have been especially close, considering both were deeply devoted Christians from the South.

Carter served as honorary chairman of Graham's 1973 crusade in Atlanta. After Carter stunned the nation and won the White House, the Carters had the Grahams to the White House as overnight guests. Amy Carter, a child, sat and watched TV.

But these two never developed the personal friendship that marked Graham's relationship with some of the other presidents. Still, he appreciated Carter's insistence on speaking out for human rights around the world. And he saw in the man from Plains, Ga., an ambassador for faith who wasn't afraid to express his devotion in

louder than his words," Rabbi Jim Bennett, then of Charlotte, said after Graham's double apology.

Years later, Graham admitted he was naïve, and that Nixon might have used the evangelist for political gain. Still, when a preacher was needed to eulogize the former president upon his death, it was Graham who got the call in 1994 in California.

There was no way Graham could pass up the chance to say good-bye to a friend — even a tainted one — and to restate the point that drove a preacher's life:

"For the believer, there is hope beyond the grave. ... Richard Nixon had that hope, and today that can be our hope as well."

GERALD FORD

They were golfing buddies.

But Graham's relationship with the President who was faced with the challenge of reuniting the nation after Nixon and Watergate went deeper than a game.

While still wanting to stay out of partisan politics, Graham sought out Ford to encourage him to pardon Nixon for the crimes of Watergate. Graham was concerned about the health and well-being of a personal friend. But as he related in a Sunday-morning call to Ford, putting Nixon through the criminal justice system

President Ronald Reagan gives the Presidential Medal of Freedom to Billy Graham at the White House in 1983.

public and to make doing the right thing part of his political platform.

The notion of a former president teaching Sunday school in his hometown and working on Habitat for Humanity houses for the poor long after he left the White House? Graham approved.

RONALD REAGAN

Graham's relationship with the Hollywood film-star-turned-world-leader was as much personal as it was political.

Their friendship dates back to the 1950s — golf brought them together, of course — and included

> *Graham was struck by Reagan's obvious wit, charm and positive spirit, and the dash he brought to the White House, as well as by his sharp political instincts.*

Graham praying at Reagan's inauguration in 1981 and again in 1985.

Graham was struck by Reagan's obvious wit, charm and positive spirit, and the dash he brought to the White House, as well as by his sharp political instincts. Graham recalled in his autobiography fancy dinners with the varied likes of Harlem Globetrotters basketball star Meadowlark Lemon and Prime Minister Margaret Thatcher of England. He remembered praying with Frank Sinatra.

Graham's friendship with this president once again gave him an entryway into politics. Despite opposition from some conservative Christians wary of Roman

Catholicism, Graham supported Reagan's decision to appoint a full ambassador to the Vatican — another hint of Graham's broadening ecumenical spirit that flourished with age.

This relationship, though, was founded largely on their friendship.

When Reagan was shot and nearly died in 1981 outside a Washington hotel, Graham got the news from then-Sen. Jesse Helms of North Carolina, then rushed north to be with the Reagans.

He prayed with the President's family. He also prayed with the family of assailant John Hinckley.

GEORGE BUSH

The Grahams and Bushes were old friends, long before the first President Bush moved into the White House. Graham gave the invocation and benediction at the Bush inauguration after his 1988 election.

But their deep relationship, and the impact that Graham had on history through his relationship with all these presidents, was symbolized by his presence in the White House on Jan. 16, 1991.

That was the night Bush declared war in response to Iraq's invasion of Kuwait. As the first U.S. bombs flew, Bush turned to Graham at his side and asked that he pray. The Nation's Pastor asked God to give us a short war with few casualties. The next day, he led a chapel service for political and military leaders. It was called "A Program for Peace," at Graham's suggestion. He focused his message on the peace we find with God, and the peace that God can bring between nations and individuals.

Graham has emphasized over the years his effort to distance himself from politics, so Bush never sought the evangelist's advice over the first Persian Gulf War, and Graham was happy to never have given any.

"I was with him as a friend and pastor," Graham said, an explanation that served as his mantra.

BILL CLINTON

The warmth that Clinton held for Graham was clear the beautiful May night in 1996 that he spoke at a fancy Washington dinner honoring the preacher.

Billy Graham with former President and Barbara Bush.

AP PHOTO/MARK FOLEY

It was Clinton who called on Graham to try to heal the nation at the memorial service after the Oklahoma City bombing.

Graham had just been awarded the Congressional Gold Medal at the Capitol Rotunda ceremony attended by such political luminaries at that time as Vice President Al Gore and Senate leaders Bob Dole, Strom Thurmond, Jesse Helms and others. Among the celebrities present for the events that day: former teen idol (and ardent Christian) Pat Boone, Frank and Kathie Lee Gifford, radio commentator Paul Harvey and, fittingly, two presidential children — Nixon's Tricia Nixon Cox and LBJ's Lynda Johnson Robb.

I covered the formal event and all of the speeches. But I was more struck by Clinton's personal remarks that night to hundreds packed into a downtown Washington hotel ballroom.

Clinton reminisced to the dinner crowd about attending Graham's 1959 crusade in Little Rock, Ark. — a small-town Arkansas boy moved by this preacher speaking of racial reconciliation during an era of great racial tension across the land. He was 11 or so at the time, and a Sunday school teacher in his church had to drive him to Little Rock for the meetings. Clinton spoke of saving up pennies from his allowance to give to Graham's crusades, never knowing, of course, that he would grow

Billy Graham with President Clinton.

up to be a president who turned to this same evangelist for prayer and comfort.

It was Clinton who called on Graham to try to heal the nation at the memorial service after the Oklahoma City bombing. Graham said he was moved that day as he watched Bill and Hillary Clinton reach out to the victims' loved ones with soft words and strong hugs.

Graham refused to endorse Clinton or another of his good friends, Republican challenger Bob Dole, in the 1996 race won handily by Clinton. He stayed largely silent through the Monica Lewinsky sex scandal that shamed Clinton and shocked the nation, refusing to publicly condemn a friend in trouble.

Again, he wanted to avoid the partisanship that would erode his pastorate. So instead, he did what he has done for every president and friend in trouble.

He prayed for Clinton.

GEORGE W. BUSH

Graham must have smiled knowingly at the growing expressions of faith from the second President Bush.

After the terrorist attack of Sept. 11, 2001, and in the midst of the conflict with Saddam Hussein and Iraq, Bush spoke more publicly about his belief that we are all connected through God.

"We Americans have faith in ourselves, but not in ourselves alone," Bush said in his State of the Union address to Congress. "We do not claim to know all the ways of Providence, yet we can trust in them, placing our confidence in the loving God behind all of his life and all of history."

What does this have to do with the pastor to the presidents?

Though Graham honors the privacy of those he counsels too much to talk, the evangelist is widely credited with leading Bush toward his life of faith.

The son of a president who was restless at times in that role, Bush admits to having been a hard-living, sometimes hard-drinking, guy from Texas. Then, in 1985, he took several walks with Graham at his parents' vacation home in Kennebunkport, Me., where they spoke of more important things.

"It was the beginning of a new walk where I would recommit my

Billy Graham with President George W. Bush.

heart to Jesus Christ," Bush wrote in his 1999 autobiography, *George W. Bush: A Charge to Keep*. "I was humbled to learn that God sent His Son to die for a sinner like me."

A year later, on July 27, 1986, during a vacation in Colorado Springs, Colo., Bush took his last sip of alcohol. His faith had begun to blossom, thanks in part to Graham.

BARACK OBAMA

By the time Obama took office, Graham's advancing years and fragile health made it difficult for the two men to forge and sustain a relationship. And yet, in April of 2010, Obama became the 12th president to meet with Graham, and the first sitting president to visit the evangelist's home in Montreat. Clearly, Graham's spiritual support still mattered to those faced with making world-changing decisions.

Obama and Graham, 91 at the time, spent 35 minutes together, along with Franklin Graham. Over coffee, they talked about golf, their families and Chicago, Obama's home and the metropolitan area where Graham graduated from college (Wheaton). Obama told Graham how humbling the office of president can be. Graham presented the president with two Bibles – one for him and one for his wife, Michelle.

In the 2012 presidential election, Graham all but endorsed Mitt Romney, a conservative whose position on such social issues as gay marriage and abortion more closely mirrored those of evangelical Christians. But that didn't keep the frail evangelist from making a solemn promise to Obama that April day two years before his reelection, when the 12th president to make his acquaintance came calling.

The evangelist prayed for the president, and the president prayed for him.

Billy Graham with President Obama.

JOHN D. SIMMONS/THE CHARLOTTE OBSERVER

Billy Graham, with former North Carolina Sen. Jesse Helms, after winning the Congressional Gold Medal in 1996.

A KINDER, GENTLER EVANGELIST

As age began taking a toll, I saw a side of Billy Graham I hadn't known until his hair was white and his health more fragile.

It's the side he began showing all of us at the end of the 20th Century and into the 21st Century — the vulnerable, often ailing and unfailingly human dimension that tended to get lost in his younger days of electrifying sermons, packed crusades, political influence and world acclaim.

To you and me, he wasn't just a long, lean, striking evangelist who preached the awesome power of Christ and had the ear of presidents. He grew to become a sweet old man who preached the tender love of Christ.

His words upon accepting the Congressional Gold Medal at a ceremony in Washington in 1996 gave a hint as to how he had begun to love people — not as great masses to be preached to, but as individuals with whom to connect one at a time.

"I wish Ruth and I had time to sit and talk to you," he said at

Congressional Gold Medal Ceremony

Honoring

Dr. and Mrs. Billy Graham

Capitol Rotunda

2:00 p.m.

May 2, 1996

the close of his message to the nation's most powerful political leaders gathered in the Rotunda of the U.S. Capitol. "I ought to be in your living room having a cup of tea. All of you are special. You have special gifts from God."

Billy Graham's Golden Age was truly golden.

As I mentioned briefly in the acknowledgments, I saw this warmer, gentler side when Graham would come to Charlotte to receive an honor or conduct some business. His aides would quietly signal me to break away from the pack of reporters and come back to a private area for a private moment. From his seat — it was hard for him to rise

out of a chair at this point — he'd reach out to embrace me. His eyes would brighten with recognition as mine brightened at the thought that he cared for me personally. That was always the essence of his ministry: He made people feel as if he cared for them, one soul at a time.

He'd ask about my family. I'd ask him to send my very best to Mrs. Graham. He'd mention something about the event that brought him to Charlotte. And then, with his aides itching to move us on, we'd say good-bye until the next occasion.

Years ago, when the often-ailing Ruth Graham was hospitalized at the world-renowned Mayo Clinic in Rochester, Minn., where the

Grahams often went for medical care, our family came home to find a message on the answering machine.

Our daughter, Ellen, 11 or 12 at the time, hit the "Play" button — and it was Billy Graham giving us a detailed update on how she was faring. The message has long been erased; the memory and the lesson behind it lives on for us.

At such a wonderfully surprising moment rich with insight into a man, this was no great preacher releasing a statement through his aides. It was a kindly, frightened old fellow who picked up the phone and returned a call on his own because he wanted to talk about the love of his life. By convincing me, he wanted to convince himself that she would be all right.

This wasn't just a man who grew sweeter with age. The broader, more humane side of Graham began shaping his ministry in many concrete, sometimes controversial ways.

While Graham was criticized in some quarters for not speaking out more boldly during the Civil Rights

> *This wasn't just a man who grew sweeter with age. The broader, more humane side of Graham began shaping his ministry in many concrete, sometimes controversial ways.*

Movement, he did what he could as a conservative Christian from the South. He invited his friend, Dr. Martin Luther King Jr., to lead a prayer at his landmark crusade in 1957 in New York's Madison Square Garden. He insisted that his crusades through the 1960s and beyond be open to people of all colors.

In 1994, Graham stated his passion for brotherhood in a personal way — he endorsed the concept of

Ruth and Billy Graham on their 50th wedding anniversary.

interracial marriage in a *Life* magazine interview.

"Integration is the only solution," Graham said. "We've got to be totally integrated — in our homes, in our worship services, even in marriage."

Later, through an aide, he told me: "I don't see anything wrong with interracial marriage. There is nothing in the Bible to forbid it. It comes down to a practical matter in today's culture."

Remember, this is a child of the segregated South, a pastor whose constituency flinched when he used the Bible to make a case sure to run counter to many people's values. But it didn't matter. This was who Graham had begun to be.

Graham biographer William Martin of Rice University in Houston said as much after the *Life* magazine article: "The remarkable thing about him is his life is becoming more and more inclusive."

He showed off that spirit of inclusiveness again early in 2000.

The Southern Baptist Convention — the denomination to which Graham belonged — had incited a national furor with plans to send missionaries to Chicago later that year to try to convert Jews, Hindus and others. A faith build on aggressive evangelism, the Southern Baptists had sparked quite a bit of anger by publishing prayer guides during the holy days of other faiths, pushing people to accept Jesus. Many Jewish, Muslim and inter-faith religious groups offered formal protests to the Southern Baptist strategies, arguing that it crossed over from evangelism to disrespecting other ways to believe.

Graham distanced himself from the Southern Baptists, refusing to cross that thin line between offering Jesus as the only hope and telling people they are doomed to eternal hell if they don't agree and accept.

"I normally defend my denomination, I'm loyal to it," he told a national TV interviewer on Fox News. "But I have never targeted Muslims. I have never targeted Jews. I believe that we should declare the fact that God loves you, God's willing to forgive you, God can change you, and Christ and his kingdom is open to anybody who repents and by faith receives him as Lord and savior."

About a year later, Graham refused to budge from this gentle stance of refusing to say something

Dr. Martin Luther King Jr. with Billy Graham.

> *"We come together today to affirm our conviction that God cares for us, whatever our ethnic, religious or political background may be."*

negative about others — even in the face of a national storm provoked by son Franklin.

Soon after the terrorist attack of Sept. 11, 2001, Franklin Graham told a Charlotte freelance interviewer during a Q&A in the N.C. mountains that Islam is "a very evil and a very wicked religion." The interview quickly aired nationwide, and the younger Graham refused to back away from his conviction, even in the face of condemnation from many.

In his book, *The Name*, Franklin Graham wrote, "The God of Islam is not the God of the Christian faith. The two are different as lightness and darkness."

Billy Graham, of course, wouldn't publicly disagree with his son — who is younger, more blunt, more willing to roll up his sleeves and duke it out.

Franklin Graham spokesman Mark DeMoss at the time said this to the *Washington Post* about Franklin: "I don't think I would describe him as confrontational. He is neither seeking controversy nor is he doing what his dad did — going to great lengths to avoid it. He's just direct. He is what he is. His attitude is, 'This is the message. I realize it will

Billy Graham preaching in 1992.

offend some and maybe others will embrace it.'"

Billy Graham, in his later years, approached faith differently.

In the message he delivered at the National Day of Prayer and Remembrance service at the National Cathedral in Washington three days after the terrorist attack of Sept. 11, Graham spoke of a God who comforts us all:

"We come together today to affirm our conviction that God cares for us, whatever our ethnic, religious or political background may be. The Bible says that he is the God of all comfort, who comforts us in all our troubles."

Graham had to be helped to the pulpit that day before a worldwide audience. But when he got there, he spoke to unite a troubled nation, not divide it.

In a society that rightfully reveres the aged, much of the later years of Graham's ministry has been tinged with nostalgia. Most everything he did, and most everything that happened to him, is viewed through the positive prism of time. We know his time is slipping away, and so each achievement, personal illness or ministry decision has greater poignancy.

Never one to keep his various illnesses to himself, Graham has had a lot of medical updating to share in these final years.

He revealed to a Philadelphia crusade audience in 1992 that he had been diagnosed with Parkinson's, a nonfatal disease of the central nervous system that left him with a halting gait and shaking hands. The disease — which he first learned he had in 1989 — chal-

lenged him. It didn't rob him of his mental sharpness, but made it difficult for him to walk, write and stand tall at the pulpit. In his final crusades, a chair was kept at the

podium should he need such relief.
He always tried to remain standing until the end.

Each time I'd see Graham and ask how he was doing, he'd share

1966.

Spirit has defined Graham's later years — a calmness that comes when you put your life and death in God's hands, and practice what you've always preached.

news of his latest medicine and side effect from Parkinson's. You could see his hands shake. It was tough on him, and those around him. But like so many other older folks struck by Parkinson's or Alzheimer's, he struggled forward.

He collapsed and nearly died from a bleeding colon while leading a crusade in Toronto in June 1995. "It was critical," Franklin Graham told me at the time. "He lost about a third of his blood. Anytime you lose that kind of blood, it's critical. If you can't stop it, you're going to bleed to death."

But, again, life went on. He got out of a hospital bed and preached

to a stadium-record crowd of 73,500 on the last night of his crusade at the Toronto SkyDome.

He fell three times in 1995, once on some shampoo while showering in a hotel room in New York City, where he had gone to accept an American Bible Society award. He fractured a rib and severely bruised his right shoulder, but he kept on going again.

After the accidents, attributed to Parkinson's, Franklin Graham said his father had the strength of an old mule, and that a fall or two wouldn't be enough to stop him.

In June of 2000, he was hospitalized at the world-famous Mayo Clinic in Minnesota when doctors discovered fluid on his brain. That one required medicine that later would leave him numb from head to toe. That same month, a series of hip-replacement procedures forced Ruth Graham to be confined to their home in Montreat. Her later years were spent at home, then often in bed.

When she died in 2007 at their home in Montreat, she was surrounded by loved ones, including the husband whose heartbreak was tempered by his belief that she went straight to heaven.

Even in his wife's illness, Graham found a deeper meaning: It reminded him that every minute is a gift from God, he said.

Even then, Graham believed: "Whatever is happening, the Lord allowed it. I have no doubt she'll be all right."

Ruth Graham's spirit was the source of inspiration to all.

Each time you'd ask one of the Graham children how their mother

CHRISTOPHER A. RECORD/THE CHARLOTTE OBSERVER

was faring, they'd smile and shake their heads and say something like, "Mama's not doing well physically, but nothing can claim her spirit."

Ruth Graham's spirit was there for all to see that Saturday afternoon in Montreat after she died in 2007, when her memorial service was filled not just with tears but with laughter from the memories.

Spirit has defined Graham's later years — a calmness that comes when you put your life and death in God's hands, and practice what you've always preached.

Graham is almost always asked about death on those occasions when he gives an interview or appears in the news. His answer is invariably the same.

"I'm looking forward to death," he told *Life* magazine in 1993. "I'll be very happy to get out of this body and into the new world that's been prepared."

There are even spiritual answers to silly questions:

"Somebody once asked me, 'Will there be golf courses in heaven?' I said, 'If they're necessary for our happiness, they'll be there.'"

The number of crusades dwindled to two or so a year. Each crusade, no matter what city served as host, was always marked by a hold-your-breath anticipation as to whether he could pull it off. He always promised he'd go as long as God allowed him to, and that's what he did with his crusades, until the

last one in 2005 in New York.

But in between the carefully staged events for which he could summon the required energy, there were fewer public appearances, and fewer pronouncements when the press called his office seeking a comment on this issue or a prayer for that crisis.

And so when he did leave his Montreat home to re-enter the spotlight, the spotlight shined ever more brightly.

In the fall of 1996, he returned to his hometown of Charlotte for one last Carolinas crusade. More than 300,000 people, as I shared earlier in this work, came to sing and pray and honor a native son.

In the spring of 1997, he published the long-awaited story of his

Rev. Billy Graham speaks at the dedication of the Billy Graham Library in May 2007.

TODD SUMLIN/THE CHARLOTTE OBSERVER

The Billy Graham Library in Charlotte.

life — *Just As I Am: The Autobiography of Billy Graham*. With a first printing of 1 million, the book became a bestseller in hardback and paperback.

In keeping with a spirit of never wanting to anger anyone, the 760-page work contains no gossipy revelations or stirring stances. "I'm not going to break confidences," he pledged before its publication. Rather, it's a blow-by-blow account of a long, rich life — an account he'd just as soon not have written.

Each time I'd ask how it was going, he'd shake his head as if to say, "Not well." He agonized over the details he spoke into a tape recorder, which then went to a team of typists, researchers and editors. His late brother, Melvin, a farmer, developer, Christian

speaker and all-around priceless fellow from the Charlotte area, recalled getting a phone call during this long journey of book-writing.

Billy Graham wanted to know how the family milk bottles were labeled years ago — Graham Brothers or Graham Brothers'.

On a cold, rainy October day in 2002, another great moment dripped with nostalgia.

Billy and Franklin Graham joined N.C. Gov. Mike Easley, Charlotte Mayor Pat McCrory and 550 other civic, business, political and religious leaders in breaking ground on the Billy Graham Evangelistic Association in Charlotte. Just off the Billy Graham Parkway, no less.

The groundbreaking marked the

move of Graham's ministry from Minneapolis to his hometown and put an end to the question he always got: Why was his ministry based in an office building on the edge of downtown Minneapolis anyway?

Because that's where he was working as president of Northwestern Schools when he founded the Billy Graham Evangelistic Association in 1950.

Charlotte — the place of his birth, a city of 700 churches, a community that has always embraced the Grahams — seemed so much more appropriate.

The new Graham home isn't just an office building on a 63-acre wooded site where 400 employees will do the evangelist's business. It includes a Billy Graham Library

BILLY GRAHAM EVANGELISTIC ASSOCIATION

At home in 1996.

that houses some of the evangelist's keepsakes and is drawing more people than almost any other tourist attraction besides of the Carolinas beaches.

When the library was dedicated in spring 2007, there were smiles, hymns, prayers and speeches from three ex-Presidents at an extraordinary ceremony: George H.W. Bush, Jimmy Carter and Bill Clinton. But even surrounded by such historic figures, Graham remained the focus for the 1,500 supporters at the dedication and thousands more watching on TV. This was his day, his legacy. He shared his love for Ruth, who was too ill to attend and would succumb just days later. Then he shared his other abiding love, delivered from a pulpit under a tent

> *It was never his crusades or memoirs that Graham cared about most when it came to the impact of his life. It is his family.*

— not unlike the tent that started it all in Los Angeles some 60 years earlier : "My whole life has been to please the Lord and honor Jesus."

But it was never his crusades or memoirs that Graham cared about most when it came to the impact of his life.

It won't just be the ministry he nurtured or the buildings he put up in Charlotte that will serve as perhaps his most powerful legacy.

It is his family.

The Grahams had five children, all adults now, who cared for their parents and stood beside them always. There are the three children content to stay largely behind the scenes — Ned, Gigi and Ruth (known to everyone as "Bunny"). Then there are the two likely to earn more of the attention now.

In the different styles of Franklin Graham and Anne Graham Lotz, a father found two to carry on the family tradition.

The furor sparked by Franklin Graham's view of Islam reflected the fiery side of the man chosen to lead the Billy Graham Evangelistic Association into the 21st Century and beyond.

It's not just that he holds a provocative view; it's that he feels called to share it no matter how many others it might make cringe.

"If I don't speak out," he once told me, "I think God will judge me. It's not that I intend to be more willing to do it. I guess it's just the way I'm wired."

A rebel child who leaned once upon a time to loud music, fast cars and cigarettes, he finally came to faith in 1974, at age 22, in a Jerusalem hotel room, after his father said it was time to make a choice in life. He cleaned up his act after that and dove into a life of ministry, but never lost touch with his rebel side.

He offers political opinions with little hesitation. He challenges

AP PHOTO

Billy Graham congratulates his son, Franklin and Franklin's wife Jane, after ordaining him.

Franklin Graham at the Samaritan's Purse warehouse.

T. ORTEGA GAINES/THE CHARLOTTE OBSERVER

authority. He electrifies the Christian community with his Operation Christmas Child campaign, which hands out millions of shoe boxes stuffed with gifts and notes for needy children.

He continues to maintain a home in rural Boone in the North Carolina mountains, partly so he can ride his motorcycle and shoot his guns in the woods in peace. He prefers jeans and cowboy boots; when he appears in a suit and tie on one of the cable TV

Franklin Graham has continued his father's crusade tradition by holding what he calls festivals all over the world.

news shows to articulate a conservative Christian view, I have to look twice to make sure it's really him. He recruits rock star Bono of supergroup U2 to join him in the fight against HIV/AIDS. He criticizes churches for allowing its disdain of homosexuality to keep some Christians from showing love to people dying of the disease.

"We want these children to know there is a God, and he loves them very much," Graham said at an Operation Christmas Child event in Charlotte, where he preached about the need to do God's work on behalf of HIV/AIDS victims. "I hope for a

Rev. Franklin Graham speaking at the dedication of YMCA Camp Harrison.

moment this will put a little joy in their lives."

Franklin Graham has continued his father's crusade tradition by holding what he calls festivals all over the world. The venues are smaller, and so are the crowds — after Billy Graham, there likely will never be a preacher to fill an 80,000-seat stadium. But Franklin Graham's festival agenda is the same — music, a message and then the altar call.

Franklin Graham has said he'll keep up the preaching and public appearances, and it's obvious he's not afraid to make tough decisions, like moving the ministry from Minneapolis to Charlotte.

But all you have to do is ask him and he'll tell you where his Christian heart lies — in the

gutters of the world's most poverty-stricken regions, with the most desperate, needy people in the world. That's where you can expect him to take his father's association now and in the future.

Anne Graham Lotz is the quiet child, one whose more reflective brand of ministry resonates with the Christian community in a different way.

She has called her worldwide gatherings "Just Give Me Jesus" rallies and her organization AnGeL Ministries for good reason.

"Anne's whole desire is, in this case, to revive or re-energize or re-spark those of us who are Christians," Ruth Snyder of suburban Charlotte told me before Lotz drew thousands to her rally at the

Anne Graham Lotz in 1999.

LAURA MUELLER/THE CHARLOTTE OBSERVER

Evangelist Anne Graham Lotz speaking at Ruth Graham's funeral in 2007.

TODD SUMLIN/THE CHARLOTTE OBSERVER

Charlotte Coliseum in 2002.

Much of Lotz's story is familiar: She became a force in conservative Christian evangelism despite having an audience of men literally turn their backs on her once because they believed the pulpit was for men only. The challenge of being a woman in a man's world was brought home again in a *Christianity Today* magazine article entitled "Angel in the Pulpit." Listening to Lotz, one man said, is like listening to Billy Graham in a skirt. Apparently he meant it as a compliment.

While she condemns homosexuality and abortion, that's

not at the top of Lotz's agenda. Her calling is as a serious teacher of the Bible, and her agenda is to stand tall at the podium — a striking figure she is, reminding one of another tall, angular evangelist — and to preach what her father preached for so long.

At the revival in Charlotte — free of charge, with only a gentle solicitation of funds — the Raleigh wife and mother stood behind a giant wooden cross and spoke of what drives her life as a child of the Grahams:

"The cry of my heart was 'Just Give Me Jesus,'" she said, recalling a two-year period of stress when she turned to her faith. "I can't get him out of my mind, and I can't take him out of my heart."

Talking to Franklin Graham, you have to make sure you don't run out of ink in your pen for all that he wants to say.

Talking to his older sister, you must pull the words out of her; she'd rather be preaching on a Bible text to an audience of faithful women than generating sound bites for headline-seeking reporters.

And yet each child will carry on the Graham name in his or her own way, infused with a respect for their father and a pride at having the privilege of being a Graham.

And like their father in his prime, there is a sense of joy and fun at the wonder of this all.

I'll never forget interviewing Lotz one morning in a hotel lobby before the groundbreaking for her father's ministry move to Charlotte. Who should wander by but her brother.

He spotted us and immediately got that mischievous look in his eye — the one that led him to name his

1995 memoir *Rebel With A Cause*. He kissed his sister on the cheek, looked at me and said: "Ask her the hard questions, too."

Everyone laughed.

In the end, though, there was more to Billy Graham than his work and the children who will keep it going.

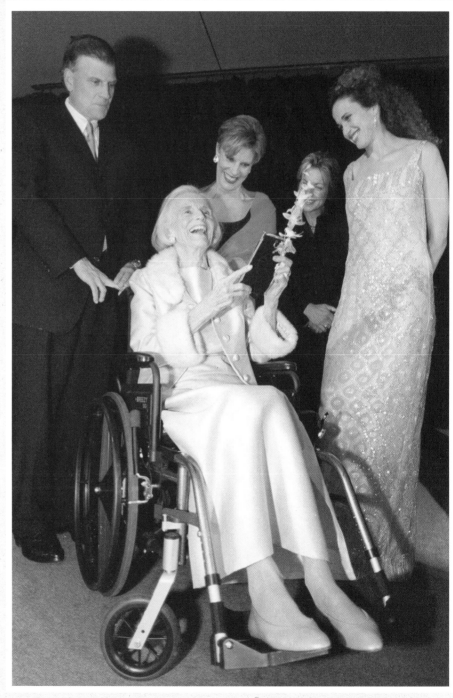

Ruth Bell Graham, seated in wheelchair, laughs as her son Rev. Franklin Graham, left, daughter Gigi Graham Tchvidjian, second from left, novelist Patricia Cornwell, third from left, and actress Andie MacDowell celebrate Graham's 80th birthday. Ruth Graham passed away in 2007.

AP PHOTO/ALAN MARLER

There was always his wife.

And there was the love they had for each other — a love that endured time and illness and separation and fame, and inspired who knows how many other people to devote their lives to their soulmate.

Ruth Graham made me smile every time I had the privilege of encountering her.

I remember the news conference where she spoke before her husband's 1998 crusade at Raymond James Stadium in Tampa, Fla. In the midst of questions and answers from reporters she didn't know, she shot me a mischievous smile and a wave, as if to say "Hey!" to a friend.

I remember interviewing her by telephone in 2001 after the publication of two books about her life and marriage. We made small talk that afternoon, but it was difficult for her; illness had already robbed her of her strength and zest. And so I wrote about the two works — *Footprints of a Pilgrim* and *Never Let it End* — without her comments, but with her words, charm and lifelong devotion moving me.

This is the heart of one of the poems about her husband that she shared with the world: "My love has long been yours — since on that day when we first met — I will never quite forget how you just paused and smiled a bit, then calmly helped yourself to it."

The encounter I'll most remember came on May 30, 2000 — a candlelit night at the famous Grove Park Inn in Asheville that celebrated two people and one union.

It was a star-studded dinner gathering graced by the presence of mystery writer Patricia Cornwell and actress Andie MacDowell, both friends of the Grahams. Cornwell, in fact, was all but raised by the Grahams in Montreat. They love her like a daughter, even if they once confessed to me that her best-selling books are a tad too gory for their taste.

The $250-a-plate, black-tie dinner raised more than $2 million for

Billy and Ruth Graham had a love to affirm and a partnership to sustain until their time together was up.

the Ruth and Billy Graham Children's Health Center in Asheville.

We dined on salmon and marinated chicken.

But the evening centered on a celebration of Ruth Graham's 80th birthday just days away. That explained the 80 orchids from her husband, the program of reminiscences and the guest of honor having to get dressed up in a cream-colored gown. Knowing her, she'd just as soon have been home in Montreat with her Bible.

But there she was in her wheelchair, smiling, accepting accolades, telling us she wouldn't have traded Billy for anyone she knew.

And Billy?

There was a poetic justice in his absence that night. Just as he was gone on so many other nights, he was gone on this one, too — in Nashville, Tenn., preparing for a crusade two nights later in spectacular, new Adelphia Stadium that would draw an average of 52,500 over four nights. Just as he had done for more than a half-century, he had to show his love long distance.

Appearing live via satellite on giant video screens, Graham remembered how he never considered holding her hand on their first date way back when at Wheaton College. She was a missionary's daughter, after all.

But he knew then this was the woman to spend a lifetime with.

"You could see Christ coming out of her face in the expression she had," Graham told the crowd of 300 friends and admirers that evening in the grand ballroom.

Then he spoke directly to his wife of 56 years, his love: "My dear Ruth, you have been more than I could ever have dreamed."

In that instant, the fame, the friendship with presidents and Billy Graham's place in history did not matter.

His crusades and her books of poetry faded.

At that moment — as in so many other moments of their life together — the crowds drifted away and the sermons were put aside. The lost and lonely of the world would have to wait for just a moment.

Billy and Ruth Graham had a love to affirm and a partnership to sustain until their time together was up.

That is what they did that night in Asheville, and every other night of a life together that slipped away much too fast.

Billy and Ruth Graham in 1997 with their five children (from left): Gigi, Anne, Ruth (Bunny), Franklin and Ned.

BILLY GRAHAM, AND TIME

For Billy Graham, as it does for the rest of us, time has moved swiftly.

In 2005, he held his last crusade, drawing 230,000 to the site of the old World's Fair on a sunbaked spring weekend in New York. I was there, and remember Graham's brief sermons, and the trouble he had commanding the lectern for any length of time. I also remember the stunning diversity of the crowd, people seemingly from every culture and country on this great earth, united by their faith and hope. After the last "Amen," he retreated largely to life out of the limelight in Montreat, with his wife, Ruth. In the spring of 2007, though frail, he addressed an invitation-only crowd of 1,500 friends and dignitaries gathered for the dedication of the Billy Graham Library in Charlotte. The gathering included Presidents (and friends) George Bush, Jimmy Carter and

John McCain, Mitt Romney and Sarah Palin; publication of a few books; plans late in 2013 for an evangelical blitz entitled My Hope America with Billy Graham, combining videos with Christians opening their homes for visits centered around discovering Christ. His 90th birthday in 2008 inspired a party for 160 family and friends with barbecue, fried chicken and sweet tea. His ministry received 100,000 birthday greetings, including a video from then-President Bush.

His ministry has done a masterful job keeping Graham in the forefront, at least on the website, in print and through recycled crusade footage. Every once in a while

Franklin and Billy Graham in 2007.

TODD SUMLIN/THE CHARLOTTE OBSERVER

Bill Clinton. Two weeks later, Ruth died. "Not a day goes by that I don't imagine her walking through my study door or us sitting together on our porch as we did so often, holding hands as the sun set over the mountaintops," Graham wrote. With the help of his son, Franklin, he placed a rose on her casket before she was laid to rest in a quiet spot beside the Billy Graham Library in Charlotte. He will be laid to rest beside her when the time comes, softly played hymns piped into the area, benches nearby for visitors to come and pay their respects, and to reflect on the meaning of it all.

There has been the occasional "public moment" in the years since — a well-chronicled private meeting with President Obama in 2010; visits (always publicized by the PR people!) with politician/candidates

Billy Graham delivering a prayer in 2005.

TODD SUMLIN/THE CHARLOTTE OBSERVER

Former Presidents George H. Bush, Bill Clinton and Jimmy Carter with Rev. Billy Graham and Franklin Graham in May 2007.

channel-surfing, I'll come across a TV show airing a vintage Billy Graham crusade from the 1950s or 1960s, that tall, lanky preacher breathing fire long ago.

But for the most part, day to day, life the last several years for

Graham has been tenderly quiet. An array of medical issues, including his long-standing Parkinson's disease and fluid on the brain, require closely monitored care at home and not-infrequent trips to the hospital in nearby Asheville.

Difficulty seeing, hearing and walking put an end to the reflective hikes he enjoyed near their mountaintop home. He watches the news on TV, takes naps, welcomes visits from his pastor, the Rev. Don Wilton of First Baptist Church in

Spartanburg, S.C., and keeps up with the family business during visits from son Franklin, often for Sunday lunch. His sister, Jean Ford, and her husband, Leighton, will drive up for a visit from their home in Charlotte. When it's time to go back down the mountain, *The Charlotte Observer* reported, he'll say to them, "Why do you have to go?" He'll do his best to

> Even as age has brought with it frailty, Graham has continued searching for the meaning in this life, and sought to share those teachable moments with the rest of us.

keep up with the mail, do a little business with the help of loyal staff, and work on some project, as much as he is able. But a steady stream of calls from the media — for an interview or a comment on the news of the day — is typically but politely turned down. The expectations that come with being the world's foremost evangelist have long since subsided.

And yet...

Rev. Billy Graham at his Montreat home in 1996.

Even as age has brought with it frailty, Graham has continued searching for the meaning in this life, and sought to share those teachable moments with the rest of us. Counseling, comforting, teaching — it's what he's been doing for a lifetime. Why stop now?

A poignant example of that came in 2011, when he published a book entitled Nearing Home. The fiery sermons of the past have been replaced by gentle, practical counsel offered to others late in life: Pray. Plan (i.e., preparing a will and making your medical wishes known). Stay engaged in church and community. Set some daily goals, because the devil delights in someone who is idle or bored, he warns. As he writes: "While society may not believe that growing old is a respectable phase of life, my prayer is that believers in Jesus Christ will walk the last mile of the way triumphantly, as Moses did when he died at age 120."

One hundred twenty.

If he's around at that age, or whatever age, chances are good that Billy Graham will be working on something or other, with the help of family and colleagues, as best as he is able, for the good of the cause, to God's everlasting glory.

Rev. Billy Graham speaking at the Billy Graham Library dedication in 2007.

Billy Graham reading a Bible before going on stage at a crusade.

RICH SUGG/THE KANSAS CITY STAR

THE LEGACY ENDURES

Billy Graham has spent his life leading people to God.

The power of his work is that not even death, when it comes, will diminish his legacy. Graham's influence lives on in the thousands of men, women and children whose hearts and minds his ministry touched over more than a half-century. The silver-haired evangelist preached from the world's pulpits, after all, not simply to draw big crowds, but to convince each person who came to give his or her life to Christ.

This is the most important dimension of Billy Graham's public life: Thousands of people who answered his altar calls over the years lived a more blessed life because they got out of their chair, came forward, accepted a tract, an embrace and a prayer, and then went home filled with fresh hope.

Each month that the ministry's *Decision* magazine arrives in the mail in homes and offices around the world, it is filled with words and photographs on the ministry's work, and spiritual reflections on the issues of the day. But perhaps the most telling regular feature is "Finding Jesus," in which someone who came to Christ through a Billy Graham ministry shares his or her testimony.

Graham lived and preached for Christians like Keith Wells, a former sound and lighting technician with a rock band who shared his story in the December 2004 issue of the colorful magazine.

It was 1979, and the then 19-year-old from Canada walked into the Billy Graham crusade in Halifax, Nova Scotia, with no inten-tion of giving up what he called his booze and wild ways. After the first night, Wells remained unconvinced. After the second night, his cynicism began to erode.

"On the third evening," he wrote in *Decision*, "something happened. Mr. Graham was the first person to tell me that God loved me, that God would forgive me and that I could have a better life. Even though I loved the rock 'n' roll lifestyle, something deep inside of me said, 'This is right!' I knew in my gut that something was calling me. I looked at my girlfriend, Sandra, and without a word we both stood up and went to the front to accept Christ."

How many times has that story repeated itself across the miles and the years? How many people walked

RICH SUGG/THE KANSAS CITY STAR

Billy Graham at a Kansas City Crusade.

KANSAS CITY STAR FILE PHOTO

into a Billy Graham crusade lost and walked out having found what they needed to live life to the fullest?

Wells wrote that he eventually gave up the rock band and alcohol, and wound up pastor of a church. More than that, he wound up knowing where to turn, because of directions provided by a lanky fellow from a N.C. dairy farm.

"People ask me what is different about being a Christian," Wells wrote. "I tell them that I know Whom to call when things are rough and Whom to thank when things are good."

But the stories of people saved at a crusade led by a grown-up Billy Graham aren't all that live on. There is the stunning story that came to me in the mail one morning — the story of a woman who was there the day a precocious boy from Charlotte took the first step on a journey that changed the world.

We've already reminisced about the autumn night in 1934 that Billy Graham was saved at a revival in Charlotte led by fiery traveling evangelist Mordecai Ham. In his wonderful autobiography, *Just As I Am*, Graham recalled the experience, and a teenager's worry that maybe he wasn't showing enough emotion to get saved.

"On the last verse of that second song, I responded," Graham wrote. "I walked down to the front, feeling as if I had lead weights attached to my feet, and stood in the space before the platform. That same night, perhaps three or four hundred other people were there at the front making spiritual commitments …

"My heart sank when I looked over at the lady standing next to me with tears running down her cheeks. I was not crying. I did not feel any special emotion of any kind just then. Maybe, I thought, I was not supposed to be there. Maybe my good intentions to be a real Christian wouldn't last…."

His good intentions lasted, all right, proving that a Christian can come to Christ in any instance, at any circumstance, with any emotion.

Lela Eaves Campbell ought to know. She was the one there beside Billy Graham — "the lady standing next to me with tears running down her cheeks."

I was moved to tears myself the December morning I opened Lela's letter at work and read the account of that evening from a Charlotte

"I felt God had led me to this place. I looked beside me and there stood a tall, young man with blond hair. His face was white as stone with no expression. It was Billy Graham."

woman who never let the years dull her memory. Lela was in her early 90s when she wrote me — a longtime Sunday school teacher at Charlotte's Pritchard Memorial Baptist Church who just wanted me to know a little more about that pivotal moment in her life, and in Billy Graham's:

"I am that lady that stood beside Billy Graham that cried so hard at the Dr. Ham meeting," she wrote in a letter she called "A Pleasant Memory." "The time was back in the Depression, I was married and staying back home because my husband had lost his job and I had a young baby. I was 22 years old. My mother's next-door neighbor … asked me to go with her to hear Dr.

The Rev. Franklin Graham, left, and his father, Dr. Billy Graham in 2003.

AP PHOTO/HUGH MORTON

Ham. I did not want to go because I thought I was saved and it would be a waste of time. That was the feeling I had when I went to the meeting. Dr. Ham's preaching and knowledge of the Bible kept me spellbound.

"When the invitation was given, I went down. I felt and knew I was not saved and I needed help. I was crying very hard with lots of tears. I felt God had led me to this place. I looked beside me and there stood a tall, young man with blond hair. His face was white as stone with no expression. It was Billy Graham and next to him stood (his friend) Grady Wilson who looked like he was in shock.

"We were told to go back someplace and we would be prayed for and talked with. I never knew when it was over; all I knew was that I felt wonderful for being loved by the Holy Spirit. Billy never said a word…."

It was an instant in American religious history that changed a young Charlotte boy and the thousands he would grow up to electrify — an instant preserved by a sweet Southern Baptist woman who simply wanted me to know what had happened.

A month or so after her letter arrived, I called Mrs. Campbell to get her permission to share the memory with readers. She was fighting the flu that day, so we only chatted for a few minutes. She said it would be fine to share the letter, because memories are what we cling to as the years pass by far too fast.

In this case, it's the memory of a teary-eyed girl of 22 who stood beside a boy the day he found Christ, a boy who wound up speaking on the Good Lord's behalf.

85

1961.

BILLY, IN HIS OWN WORDS

In all manner of writings, Billy Graham created a wealth of faith and wisdom that will outlive us all. Read on ...

Graham's reflection that begins his official biography prepared by the ministry sums up the belief that drives him:

"My one purpose in life is to help people find a personal relationship with God, which I believe comes through knowing Christ."

On Nov. 20, 1949 — the final night of the historic crusade in Los Angeles that catapulted him to fame — Graham closed his sermon with his trademark call to come forward and embrace Christ. Here's an excerpt that appeared in the November 2004 edition of *Decision* magazine:

"This is the last meeting of this campaign. If you're ever going to be saved, if you're ever going to be sure

you're saved, you'd better do it today. This may be the last chance you will ever have. Come. Make sure. Settle it today ... The only person who wants you in hell is the devil. He's the only one. And you know what he's doing today? He's whispering in your ear. He says, 'Don't you make a decision for Christ; you've got plenty of time.' That is the devil's big lie: 'You've got plenty of time.' But you *don't* have plenty of time...."

∞

Fifty-five years later, Graham returned to the Los Angeles area to lead a 2004 crusade that drew more than 300,000 to the Rose Bowl. The times changed, the crowds grew more diverse and the evangelist's hair grew white. But the message stayed rock-solid, as reflected in this sermon excerpt from the January 2005 edition of *Decision*:

"What about you? Have you ever been to the Cross and really opened your heart to Jesus Christ? You may be a good person, a moral person, a church person, but you are not sure that you really know Christ as your Lord and your Savior. I'm going to ask you to make that commitment to Christ. ..."

∞

His special gift was offering the comfort of Christ to those ravaged by loneliness, as this excerpt from the September 2004 edition of *Decision* simply yet powerfully illustrated:

"... To scores of people who write to our office every week, life no longer seems to be worth living.

About 11,000 people gathered at Kemper Arena for the Billy Graham Crusade Aug. 30, 1978.

A Graham Christmas card.

Jesus Christ
the same yesterday, and today,
and forever!

HEBREWS 13:8

"... As we approach the special time of year when we celebrate our Savior's birth, the story of God becoming flesh in order to redeem sinful man is still the most thrilling and powerful truth I know.

"The miraculous birth, sinless life, sacrificial death, and triumphant resurrection of Jesus Christ is what distinguishes the Christian faith from the religions of the world. When Jesus stepped out of eternity and into time

How we have appreciated
your prayers

For you, I have good news. God did not create you to be a defeated, discouraged, frustrated, wandering soul who seeks in vain for peace. He has bigger plans for you. He has a larger world and a greater life for you. The answer to your problem, however great, is as near as your Bible, as simple as first-grade arithmetic and as real as your heartbeat. ..."

For friends and supporters, it wasn't Christmas until you received the Grahams' annual card in the mail featuring a lovely portrait of Billy and Ruth at their home in Montreat, with a Bible passage to lift up the season. The association in December 2004 shared a Christmas reflection from Billy which began like this:

as a babe in a Bethlehem stable, it was the turning point for the history of mankind. God had come to earth to rescue us from our sin. …"

⌘

In a *Time* magazine profile in the edition of Nov. 15, 1993, Graham shared what he believes about the most important dimensions of Christianity:

— On God: "God does not dwell in a body, so we cannot define him in a material way. God is a spirit. I have had tremendous messages from him, which are from the Bible; it's not something I've dreamed up or had a vision of. It's important to study the Bible on a daily basis so he can speak to me."

— On Scripture: "We have to have some rule of law in theology as well as every other part of our lives, and the rule of our spiritual life is found in the Bible, which I believe was totally and completely inspired by God. Our good works come from our belief that the Bible is inspired by God, and the life of Christ is our pattern."

— On the Virgin Birth: "That is a very tender and fantastic thing. Because I believe the Bible, I believe it's important. It is not necessary for one's salvation, but as we follow Christ it's one of the cardinal points we must accept."

⌘

For all the sermons and books, it was the most personal expressions that best captured Graham's Christian belief that life doesn't end with death. After the unexpected passing of his brother, Melvin, in August 2003

in Charlotte, Billy sent this note of thanks to those who had expressed condolences to the family:

"We are deeply grateful for your kindness at Melvin's homegoing.

"I will sorely miss him as my only brother, and one of my closest friends.

"However, I know he went straight into the presence of our Lord Jesus Christ, and I look forward to seeing him again soon."

> *"God does not dwell in a body, so we cannot define him in a material way. God is a spirit. I have had tremendous messages from him, which are from the Bible…."*

After writing a personal note, I was so appreciative to receive this response from Graham, addressed to "My dear Ken":

I was deeply moved that you would take the time to write to me — it hardly seems possible that a year has gone by since my brother Melvin went home to Heaven! Thank you for thinking of me. …"

⌘

The Billy Graham I came to know is best captured in a letter our family received from him in September 2003. It's framed now, gracing a table in our family's den. I had written in August of that year about our second child, Ellen, going off to college, leaving my wife, Sharon, and I home alone now — empty-nesters facing a new kind of life. The deeper theme of the piece was about the blessings of relationships. … how getting to know people makes life rich. Within a few days, Billy's letter arrived at our Charlotte home. It spoke of the profound impact of loneliness in our lives, and the power we have to fight it. But instead of preaching to millions at a crusade, he was speaking softly to one friend.

Here's some of what he wrote to me, which is what he preached to the world, which is what we all cherish with his passing:

"It is interesting how even in the midst of activity, in a crowd of people, or watching an interesting movie — we can have a sudden sense of loneliness. I have always felt that this is actually a loneliness that only God can fill. As the Scripture says: We are fearfully and wonderfully made. There are so many things in our Christian faith that I do not pretend to understand, nor do I have quick top-of-the-head answers for. I have been rereading and studying the first three chapters of Genesis. The events are past human understanding.

"Please give my regards to Sharon. From your description, she must be a wonderful woman and a great helpmate. …

"Thank you for your friendship." He signed it "Billy."

Billy Graham talks with Sandy Berkley before visiting patients injured in the 1981 Hyatt Regency hotel disaster.

CLIFF SCHIAPPA/THE KANSAS CITY STAR

BILLY, IN OTHERS' WORDS

Whether coming from pastors, professors or a dearly departed North Carolina farmer who literally loved him like a brother, it is a privilege to read the reflections of those who have known all sides of Billy Graham. Read the words of others now, and you'll feel blessed, too.

MELVIN GRAHAM

I always considered Melvin Graham a friend. The younger brother of Billy, he was a farmer and developer from just outside Charlotte, but he was also a lay evangelist and all-around character who loved to tell a joke, wear caps, praise God and brag on his brother. He died suddenly of cardiac arrest in 2003, the day before he would have celebrated his 79th birthday. The night Melvin died, I remember his brother-in-law, evangelist Leighton Ford, sharing the sad news with me over the phone. What outlasts the tears are the happy memories, and this piece Melvin wrote exclusively for *The Charlotte Observer* a month before Billy Graham came home to Charlotte in 1996 to hold his last hometown crusade. This was no recollection of a great evangelist; it was a brother recalling a brother:

"Since everything that can be thought has been written or spoken about my brother, I thought of a time when he was about 12 or 13 years old that no one else has ever thought about.

"We, or should I say my father and uncle, operated a dairy farm on Park Road, and Billy always loved goats and dogs. I was about eight at the time and our dad bought Billy a very large brown goat with a great pair of horns. No one could get that goat to like them except Billy.

"That goat could pull a small wagon with a harness our dad got with the goat. Also, a wagon came with the purchase.

"Park Road had a narrow pavement, about eight feet wide at that time, having been an unpaved road previously. Billy would ride an old bicycle with the goat right behind him, and our collie dog behind the goat, and a little black and white nanny goat behind the dog. They would go up and down the road, and what few motorists there were would be amused.

"Some show."

"My dad later sold the big goat, harness and wagon to Wiggins Ice and Fuel Co. for advertisement purposes. When Billy got to Sharon High School, he lost interest in everything except baseball and girls — not necessarily in that order.

"When Billy was 16, our family attended the Ham-Ramsey meetings in an old wooden tabernacle on Pecan Avenue. From that time on 'til the present, he was called by the Lord to preach the gospel of Jesus Christ.

"I took over the dairy farm when I was 18 or 19 and operated it on Park Road 'til it was discontinued in 1960.

"This is a small insight into a short span of Billy's life when he lived at home on Park Road. God bless you."

T.W. WILSON

To the evangelical Christian world, he was Thomas Walter Wilson, an associate evangelist in the Billy Graham Evangelistic Association. But to Billy, he was T.W., a boyhood friend from Charlotte who walked with him on the journey from adolescence to evangelism. T.W. Wilson died in 2001, at age 82. In this piece also written for *The Charlotte Observer* in 1996, T.W. reminisced about his dear friend.

"Back in the early days before Billy Graham or I were married, we would double date. To show you the qualities

> *"He was always the top salesman. I think this is one way God has used him — he is sold on his 'product' and he knows how to sell it to the public. God gave him that gift of communication. ..."*

of the man at that time, he had a car that his daddy had given him. I didn't have a car and was about as poor as Job's turkey, living on the other side of the tracks as it were. Every other time he would have me drive the car and would always give me money to pay for the setup for our dates.

"In other words, he was always giving me the credit for doing something that I didn't do. They (our dates) thought I was setting them up, but it was Billy paying the bill.

"During the summer between school terms, Billy and my late brother Grady and I traveled in North and South Carolina selling Fuller Brushes. Grady and I tried to outsell Billy, but he was always the top salesman. I think this is one way God has used him — he is sold on his 'product' and he knows how to sell it to the public. God gave him that gift of communication. ...

"I have known Billy Graham for over 60 years. He couldn't fool me if he tried. Do you know he is more humble, more compassionate, more understanding today than at any other time I have ever known him? If there is anybody who would know his honesty, his sincereness, his integrity, his humility, it is I, because I spend so much time with him.

"He is always giving team members credit for what we really don't deserve. I think this is why so many of our team members and staff have been with Billy for so long. We know that he is for real. As we look around with hypocrisy in so many areas, even of Christian work, we are just thrilled and honored to have a small part in Billy Graham's work. It's not accidental that God has honored him and put him where he is."

PETER HOBBIE

Peter Hobbie, an ordained Presbyterian pastor who taught religion and church history for years at little Presbyterian College in Clinton, S.C., sees Billy Graham through the eyes of a scholar. But he also sees him through the eyes of a Southern boy, as he wrote here:

"I learned who Billy Graham was when my family got its first TV set. As very young Southern Presbyterians, my brothers, sister and I were fascinated by the religious healers and shouters we would find on TV. This was Southern religion as we had never heard or seen it.

"We also discovered Billy Graham as we surfed our three local channels. We knew he was Southern, too; we could tell by his accent. But he was different from the other TV evangelists. Graham sounded more like a Presbyterian.

"We didn't know it (at the time), but Graham was closer to the Southern religious tradition than any other evangelist of the 20th Century. Southern religion's strength historically rests on a broad and numerically overwhelming coalition of Protestant denominations. Billy Graham, born a Presbyterian and a converted Baptist, was a product of that coalition. As a young evangelist, he directed his appeal to this broad range of Protestant evangelical belief. ..."

GEORGE W. BUSH

Of all the stories involving Billy Graham and U.S. presidents dating back to Harry Truman, among the most powerful is the one involving George W. Bush and a stroll in Kennebunkport, Maine, in the summer of 1985. We've shared details of that encounter in this work, as it has been shared in numerous other articles and books about Bush — how Graham planted the seed of faith in his conversation with a searching

"I knew I was in the presence of a great man. He was like a magnet; I felt drawn to seek something different. He didn't lecture or admonish; he shared warmth and concern. Billy Graham didn't make you feel guilty; he made you feel loved."

— George W. Bush

Bush that day, and how Bush's life took a more serious, spiritual turn. The man who went on to become president recalled that conversation in a book titled *God and George W. Bush: A Spiritual Life*. The book by Paul Kengor, in fact, comes with this dedication: "For Billy Graham, preacher to presidents":

"I knew I was in the presence of a great man," Bush said of Graham, and their walk together. "He was like a magnet; I felt drawn to seek something different. He didn't lecture or admonish; he shared warmth and concern. Billy Graham didn't make you feel guilty; he made you feel loved."

WILLIAM MARTIN

Over the years, whenever I need to turn to someone for fresh insight into Billy Graham, I turn to my friend William Martin. The Houston professor and author wrote the definitive Graham biography — *A Prophet with Honor* — based on his nearly unlimited access to the ministry. Whenever I or another writer need to pick his brain, he is gracious with

his time and wisdom, always peeling back another layer to the story. When the highly respected *Christianity Today* magazine — the idea for which came from Graham — looked to someone to write an essay in 1995 for their cover story, "Fifty Years with Billy Graham," they looked to Martin. Here is an excerpt that gets to the heart of the meaning of it all:

"[Billy] Graham's ability to speak to American culture so successfully for 50 years stems in some measure from the fact that he is in many ways an apotheosis of the core values of our culture. If results are the measure, he is the best who ever was at what he does, but he attained that height through hard and honest work, not through inheritance or blind chance. Always ready to use the latest instruments of technology and media to accomplish his goals and maintain his prominence, he nevertheless insists that his most valuable asset has been a circle of old and loyal friends. He has walked with kings and princes and received unprecedented and sustained media attention for over four decades, but he still strikes us as something of a small-town boy, astonished that anyone would think him special."

Rev Billy Graham attending the funeral of George Beverly Shea.

A GRAHAM CATALOG

ANTHEM FOR THE AGES

A defining moment at each Billy Graham crusade came when gospel legend George Beverly Shea rose to sing the classic that inspired who knows how many Christians to stand up and proclaim "Amen!"

Enjoy now the words to "How Great Thou Art" — the song that brought sweet harmony to Graham's life and times:

O Lord my God,
When I in awesome wonder,
Consider all the worlds Thy Hands
  have made;
I see the stars, I hear the rolling thunder,
Thy power throughout the universe
  displayed.
Then sings my soul,
My Saviour God, to Thee,
How great Thou art,
How great Thou art.
Then sings my soul,
My Saviour God, to Thee,

How great Thou art,
How great Thou art!
When through the woods,
and forest glades I wander,
And hear the birds sing sweetly
    in the trees.
When I look down,
from lofty mountain grandeur
And see the brook,
and feel the gentle breeze.
Then sings my soul,
My Saviour God, to Thee,
How great Thou art,
How great Thou art.
Then sings my soul,
My Saviour God, to Thee,
How great Thou art,
How great Thou art!
And when I think,
that God, His Son not sparing;
Sent Him to die,
I scarce can take it in;
That on the Cross,
my burden gladly bearing,
He bled and died to take away
    my sin.
Then sings my soul,
My Saviour God, to Thee,
How great Thou art,
How great Thou art.
Then sings my soul,
My Saviour God, to Thee,
How great Thou art,
How great Thou art!
When Christ shall come,
with shout of acclamation,
And take me home,
what joy shall fill my heart.
Then I shall bow,
in humble adoration,
And then proclaim:
My God, how great Thou art!
Then sings my soul,
My Saviour God, to Thee,

How great Thou art,
How great Thou art.
Then sings my soul,

My Saviour God, to Thee,
How great Thou art,
How great Thou art!

The Rev. Billy Graham speaking at his wife's funeral in 2007.

THE MESSAGE ENDURES

The beauty of Billy Graham is that he delivered his message in a way any person could appreciate. Whether from the world's stage or in published works that will live on in hearts and libraries, he shared his faith in decent, direct, simple terms. See for yourself in any of his writings, available at many Christian and secular bookstores or through the ministry, at www.billygraham.org.

1947
Calling Youth to Christ

1953
I Saw Your Sons at War
Peace With God, revised and
    expanded in 1984

1955
Freedom from the Seven
    Deadly Sins
The Secret of Happiness

1958
Billy Graham Talks to Teenagers

1960
My Answer
Billy Graham Answers Your
    Questions

1965
World Aflame

1969
The Challenge

1971
The Jesus Generation

1975
Angels: God's Secret Agents

1977
How to Be Born Again

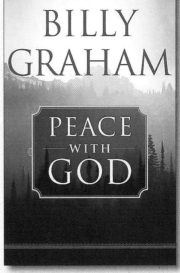

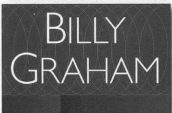

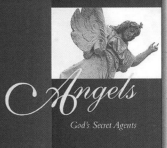

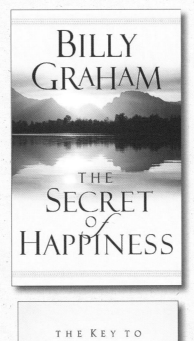

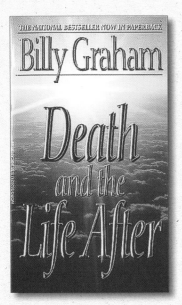

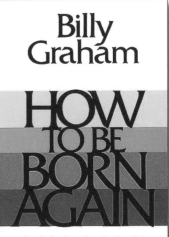

1978

The Holy Spirit

1981

Till Armageddon

1983

Approaching Hoofbeats: The Four Horsemen of the Apocalypse

1984

A Biblical Standard for Evangelists

1986

Unto the Hills

1987

Facing Death and the Life After

1988

Answers to Life's Problems

1991

Hope for the Troubled Heart

1992

Storm Warning

1997

Just As I Am

2002

Hope for Each Day

2003

The Key to Personal Peace

2005

Living in God's Love: The New York Crusade

2006

The Journey

2008

Wisdom for Each Day

2010

Storm Warning

2011

Nearing Home

2012

The Heaven Answer Book

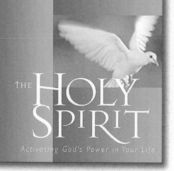

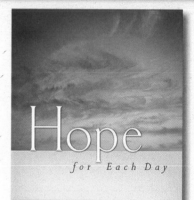

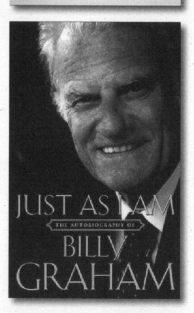

PRAYER FOR THE PRESIDENT

On a cold winter's day in January 2005, a Great American Tradition continued in Washington: Billy Graham participated in his ninth presidential inauguration, this one for the second term of George W. Bush.

Graham had first joined in the nation's great celebration of freedom in 1965, when he preached at a service the day president Lyndon Baines Johnson took office. Forty years later, age, Parkinson's disease and other issues wouldn't allow Graham to climb the U.S. Capitol steps and pray in the bitter cold at the swearing-in for his longtime family friend.

So the next morning, in the spectacular National Cathedral, at the final inaugural event for Bush, Graham opened the National Prayer Service with a moment or two of reflection for a sanctuary full of dignitaries. The 90-minute service was broadcast live on C-SPAN. The great Irish tenor Ronan Tynan opened the service with a stirring "How Great Thou Art," how appropriate since that is the anthem so identified with a Graham crusade. Then the silver-haired evangelist used a walker on rollers to get to the podium, where he shared this short yet poignant message:

The 55th Presidential Inaugural Prayer Service Jan. 21, 2005.

AP PHOTO/SUSAN WALSH

Rev. Billy Graham gives his prayer during the 55th Presidential Inaugural Prayer Service Jan. 21, 2005.

AP PHOTO/SUSAN WALSH

"Our Father and our God, we thank you that the last event of this historic week is a time of worship — a time to hear your word, to pray and to declare our dependence on you.

"In the quietness and calmness of this great cathedral, turn us away from everything that would distract us, and help us to focus on our need of you. We remember that it is written in the Scriptures, 'Unless the Lord builds the house, its builders labor in vain.'

"Our Father, we acknowledge your divine help in the selection of our nation's leaders throughout our history, and we believe that in your providence you have granted a second term of office to our President, George W. Bush, and our Vice President, Richard Cheney. Their next four years are hidden from us — but they are not hidden from you. You know the challenges and opportunities they will face. Give them a clear mind and a warm heart, calmness in the midst of turmoil, reassurance in times of discouragement and your presence always.

"We pray for their families, and we ask for your protection and care for them during the pressures of these next four years.

"Renew our vision, restore our faith and rekindle our desire to love and to serve all humanity. May we never forget that one day we each will stand before you to give an account of what you have entrusted to us.

"Finally, our Father, we pray for our nation and our world. We thank you for those who have sacrificed their lives to give us our freedom, and we pray for those who continue to serve our nation in places of great conflict and danger. Above all, we join today with millions of others across this torn and confused world in praying for peace.

"Thank you for the overwhelming compassion that our leadership and our country have shown toward the suffering in southeast Asia.

"And now may this service become a time of commitment for each one of us, as we rededicate ourselves to you and your will for our lives.

"This I pray in the name of our Lord and Savior, Jesus Christ.

"Amen."

Then, leaning still on his walker, Graham walked slowly back to his seat.

FOREVER ADMIRED

Spiritually at least, it became an American rite.

Nearly each year that the Gallup Organization released its list of the Ten Most Admired Men, there was the name Billy Graham beside presidents, popes and statesmen.

He has been named in the annual survey of everyday Americans 56 times since 1955, more than any other man. Ronald Reagan appeared on the Top 10 List 31 times before his death in 2004. Pope John Paul II and Presidents Carter, Eisenhower, Nixon, Clinton, and Truman each made 20 or more appearances.

Billy Graham has been on the Top 10 Most Admired List of men 56 times since 1955, more than any other man.

Billy Graham's 1972 crusade in Charlotte, N.C.

CHARLOTTE OBSERVER FILE PHOTO

THE WORLD WAS HIS STAGE

From Aarhus in Denmark to Zurich in Switzerland, millions flocked to stadiums, arenas, parks and other venues over the decades, in search of God's words, delivered by God's messenger. Here is where Billy Graham led his crusades:

1947
Charlotte, North Carolina
Grand Rapids, Michigan

1948
Augusta, Georgia
Modesto, California

1949
Altoona, Pennsylvania
Baltimore, Maryland
Los Angeles, California
Miami, Florida

1950s

AP PHOTO

1950

Atlanta, Georgia
Columbia, South Carolina
Minneapolis, Minnesota
New England States Tour
Boston, Massachusetts
Portland, Oregon

1951

Cincinnati, Ohio
Southern States Tour
Fort Worth, Texas
Shreveport, Louisiana
Greensboro, North Carolina
Memphis, Tennessee
Raleigh, North Carolina
Hollywood, California
Seattle, Washington

1952

Albuquerque, New Mexico
Houston, Texas
Jackson, Mississippi
Pittsburgh, Pennsylvania
American Cities Tour (Apr./May)
American Cities Tour (Aug.)
Washington, D.C.

1953

Asheville, North Carolina
Chattanooga, Tennessee
Dallas, Texas
West Texas Tour
Detroit, Michigan
Florida Cities Tour
St. Louis, Missouri
Syracuse, New York

— HUNDREDS of CHURCHES UNITING —
GREATER LOS ANGELES REVIVAL
BILLY GRAHAM
EVERY NITE 7:30 SUNDAYS 3 - 8:45
6000 free SEATS · DYNAMIC PREACHING · GLORIUS MUSIC

· CLIFF BARROWS
· BEVERLY SHEA
· BILLIE BARROWS
· GRADY WILSON
· ROSE ARZOOMANIAN
· WILMOS CSEHY

Billy Graham's 1949 crusade in Los Angeles, Calif.

CHARLOTTE OBSERVER FILE PHOTO

Billy Graham preaching in Griffith Stadium in Washington, D.C.

CHARLOTTE OBSERVER FILE PHOTO

1954
Amsterdam, The Netherlands
Berlin, West Germany
Dusseldorf, West Germany
Frankfurt, West Germany
Paris, France
London, England
Copenhagen, Denmark
Helsinki, Finland
Stockholm, Sweden

Nashville, Tennessee
New Orleans, Louisiana
U.S. West Coast Tour

1955
Aarhus, Denmark
Gothenburg, Sweden
Oslo, Norway
U.S. Service Bases Tour — West
    Germany

Dortmund, West Germany
Frankfurt, West Germany
Mannheim, West Germany
Nurnberg, West Germany
Stuttgart, West Germany
Geneva, Switzerland
Zurich, Switzerland
Paris, France
Rotterdam, The Netherlands
London, England
Scotland Cities Tour

Glasgow, Scotland
Toronto, Ontario, Canada

1956

Richmond, Virginia
Louisville, Kentucky
Oklahoma City, Oklahoma
India and Far East Tour

1957

New York City, New York

1958

Caribbean Tour
Charlotte, North Carolina
San Antonio, Texas
Fresno, California
Los Angeles, California
Sacramento, California
San Diego, California
Santa Barbara, California
San Francisco, California

1959

Adelaide, Australia

Melbourne, Australia
Sydney, Australia
Brisbane, Australia
Canberra, Australia
Hobart, Australia
Launceston, Australia
Auckland, New Zealand
Christchurch, New Zealand
Wellington, New Zealand
Indianapolis, Indiana
Little Rock, Arkansas
Wheaton, Illinois

Billy Graham's 1954 crusade in
Wembley Stadium, London.

CHARLOTTE OBSERVER FILE PHOTO

104

1960s

1960

Enugu, Nigeria
Ibadan, Nigeria
Jos, Nigeria

Kaduna, Nigeria
Lagos, Nigeria
Usumbura, Ruanda-Urundi

Accra, Ghana
Kumasi, Ghana
Nairobi, Kenya
Kisumu, Kenya
Brazzaville, Congo
Salisbury, Rhodesia
Bulawayo, South Rhodesia
Kitwe, North Rhodesia
Moshi, Tanganyika
Addis Ababa, Ethiopia
Cairo, Egypt
Jerusalem, Jordan
Monrovia, Liberia
Berlin, West Germany
Essen, West Germany
Hamburg, West Germany
Basel, Switzerland
Bern, Switzerland
Zurich, Switzerland
Lausanne, Switzerland
Rio de Janeiro, Brazil
New York City, New York
Washington, D.C.

The Graham family in New York City in 1960.

AP PHOTO

1961

Miami, Florida
Fort Lauderdale, Florida
Bradenton-Sarasota, Florida
Boca Raton, Florida
Gainesville, Florida
Cape Canaveral, Florida
Clearwater, Florida
Orlando, Florida
Tampa, Florida
Vero Beach, Florida
West Palm Beach, Florida
Jacksonville, Florida
Peace River, Florida

Billy Graham's 1961 crusade in Philadelphia, Pa.

PHILADELPHIA NEWS INQUIRER FILE PHOTO

St. Petersburg, Florida
Tallahassee, Florida
Minneapolis/St. Paul, Minnesota
Philadelphia, Pennsylvania
Glasgow, Scotland
Belfast, Ireland
Manchester, England

1962

Buenos Aires, Argentina
South America Tour (Jan./Feb.)
Redstone Arsenal, Alabama
Jacksonville, North Carolina
Raleigh, North Carolina
Chicago, Illinois
South America Tour (Sept./Oct.)

El Paso, Texas
Fresno, California
Seattle, Washington

1963

Los Angeles, California
Paris, France
Douai, France
Lyon, France
Montauban, France
Mulhouse, France
Nancy, France
Toulouse, France
Nurnberg, West Germany
Stuttgart, West Germany

1964

Birmingham, Alabama
Louisville, Kentucky
Columbus, Ohio
Boston, Massachusetts
Providence, Rhode Island
Manchester, New Hampshire
Bangor, Maine
Portland, Maine
Omaha, Nebraska
Phoenix, Arizona
San Diego, California

107

1965

Auburn, Alabama (Auburn University)
Tuscaloosa, Alabama (University of Alabama)
Tuskegee Institute, Alabama
Dothan, Alabama
Montgomery, Alabama
Denver, Colorado
Houston, Texas
Hilo, Hawaii
Honolulu, Oahu, Hawaii
Kahului, Maui, Hawaii
Lihue, Kauai, Hawaii
Seattle, Washington
Vancouver, British Columbia, Canada
Copenhagen, Denmark

1966

Berlin, West Germany
Greenville, South Carolina
London, England

1967

Great Britain
London, England
Livelink Centers, Great Britain
Turin, Italy
Zagreb, Yugoslavia
Tokyo, Japan
Kansas City, Missouri
Ponce, Puerto Rico
San Juan, Puerto Rico
Toronto, Ontario, Canada
Winnipeg, Manitoba, Canada

Billy Graham in Kansas City, Mo.

Billy Graham in Egypt.

A Maori, Billy Graham and Ruth
Graham in Auckland, New Zealand.

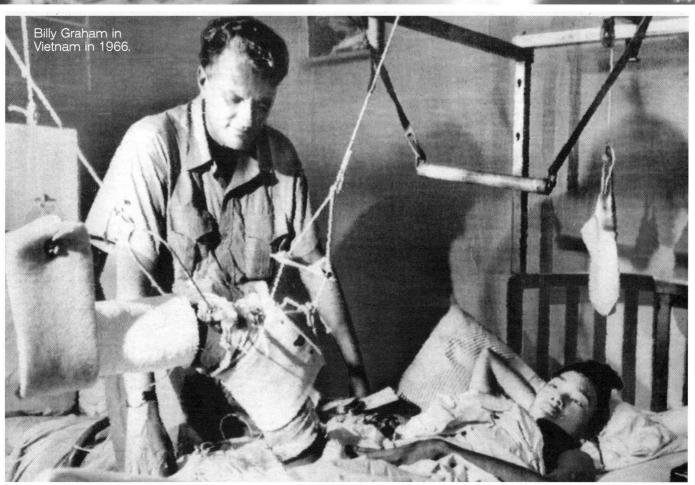

Billy Graham in Vietnam in 1966.

CHARLOTTE OBSERVER FILE PHOTO

Billy Graham in Montgomery, Ala.

AP PHOTO

1968
Pittsburgh, Pennsylvania
Portland, Oregon
San Antonio, Texas
Brisbane, Australia
Sydney, Australia

1969
Melbourne, Australia
Auckland, New Zealand
Dunedin, New Zealand
Anaheim, California
New York City, New York

1970s

1970
Baton Rouge, Louisiana
Knoxville, Tennessee
Dortmund, West Germany
New York City, New York

1971
Chicago, Illinois
Lexington, Kentucky
Dallas/Fort Worth, Texas
Oakland, California

1972
Birmingham, Alabama
Charlotte, North Carolina
Cleveland, Ohio
Kohima, Nagaland, India

Billy Graham in Hungary in 1977.

AP PHOTO

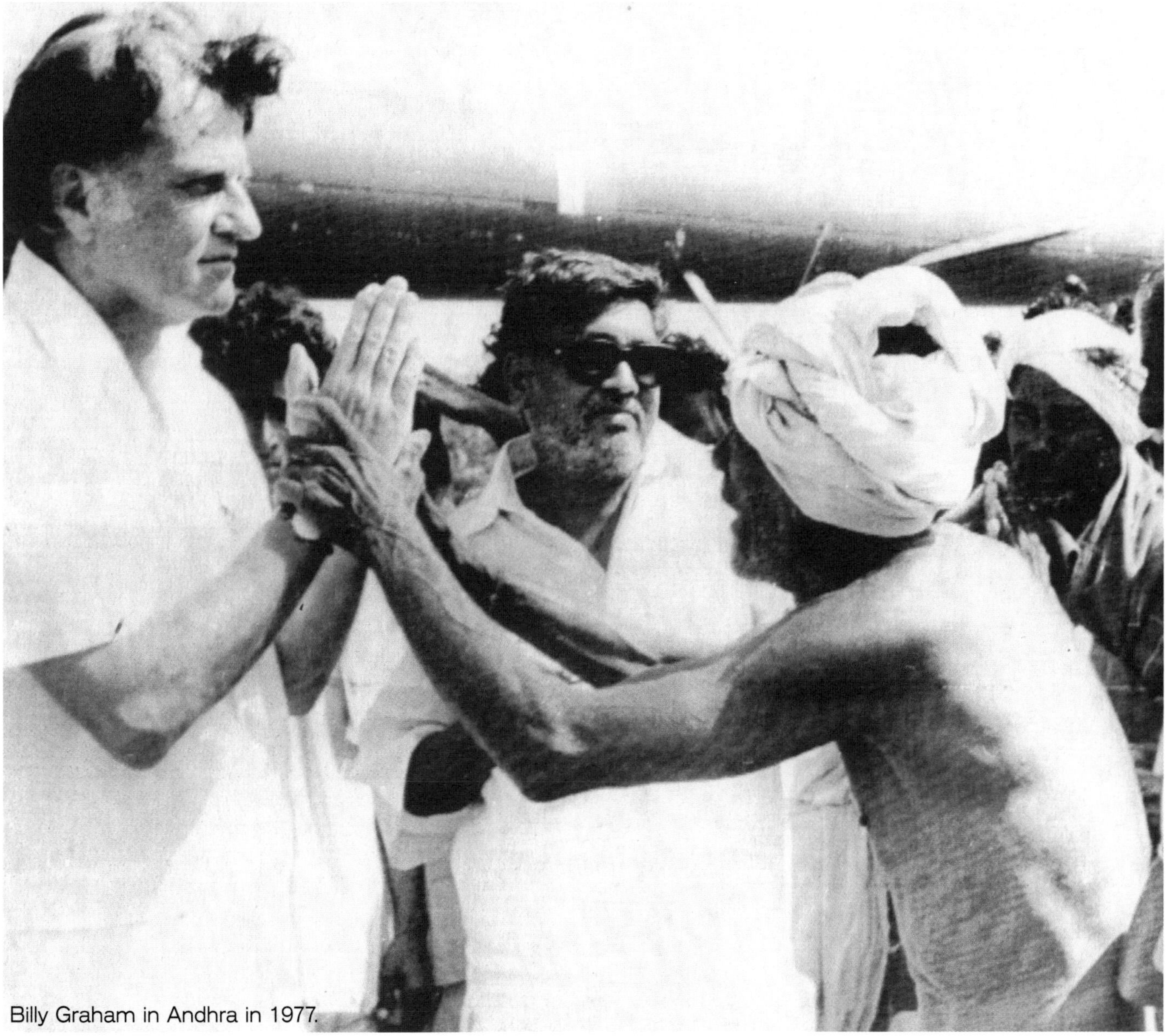

Billy Graham in Andhra in 1977.

CHARLOTTE OBSERVER FILE PHOTO

1973
Johannesburg, South Africa
Durban, South Africa
Seoul, Korea (South)
Atlanta, Georgia
Raleigh, North Carolina
St. Louis, Missouri
Minneapolis/St. Paul, Minnesota

1974
Los Angeles, California (25th
Anniversary Celebration)

Rio de Janeiro, Brazil
Phoenix, Arizona
Norfolk-Hampton, Virginia

1975
Brussels, Belgium
Albuquerque, New Mexico
Lubbock, Texas
Hong Kong
Taipei, Taiwan
Jackson, Mississippi

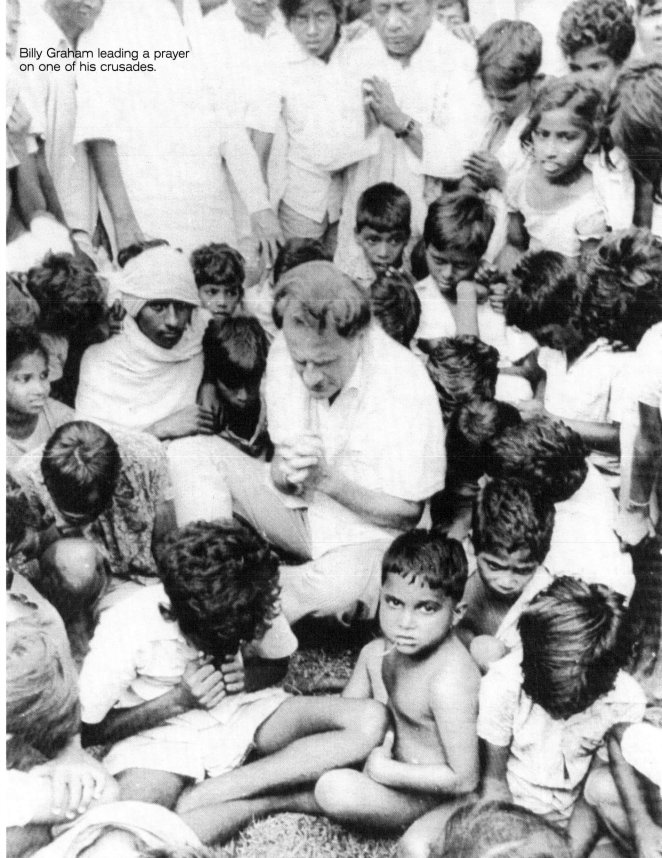

Billy Graham leading a prayer on one of his crusades.

Billy Graham in Kansas City, Mo.

1976

Nairobi, Kenya
Detroit, Michigan
San Diego, California
Seattle, Washington
Williamsburg, Virginia

1977

Hungary Tour
Gothenburg, Sweden
Manila, Philippines
Asheville, North Carolina
Cincinnati, Ohio

South Bend, Indiana
India Good News Festivals Tour

1978

Kansas City, Missouri
Las Vegas, Nevada
Memphis, Tennessee
Poland Tour
Satellite Locations in Iceland
Oslo, Norway
Satellite Locations in Norway
Stockholm, Sweden
Satellite Locations in Sweden

Singapore
Toronto, Ontario, Canada

1979

Halifax, Nova Scotia, Canada
Milwaukee, Wisconsin
Nashville, Tennessee
Sao Paulo, Brazil
Tampa, Florida
Sydney, Australia

1980

Tokyo, Japan
Okinawa, Japan
Osaka, Japan
Fukuoka, Japan
Cambridge, England
Oxford, England
Las Vegas, Nevada
Reno, Nevada
Indianapolis, Indiana
Wheaton, Illinois
Edmonton, Alberta, Canada

1981

Calgary, Alberta, Canada
Baltimore, Maryland
Boca Raton, Florida
Houston, Texas
San Jose, California
Mexico City, Mexico
Villahermosa, Mexico

1982

Hanover, New Hampshire
(Dartmouth College)

Manchester, New Hampshire
Burlington, Vermont
Portland, Maine
Hartford, Connecticut
New Haven, Connecticut
New Haven, Connecticut
(Yale University)
Amherst, Massachusetts
(University of Massachusetts)
Boston, Massachusetts
(Northeastern University)
Newton, Massachusetts
(Boston College)
South Hamilton, Massachusetts

Rev. Billy Graham speaks to
college students in 1983.

MICHAEL KODAS/THE KANSAS CITY STAR

CHARLOTTE OBSERVER FILE PHOTO

H.M. Queen Elizabeth II, Rev. Billy Graham, Ruth Graham, The Duke of Edinburgh, H.M. Queen Elizabeth The Queen Mother, and the Rector of Sandringham the Rev. Gerry Murphy.

(Gordon-Conwell Seminary)
Springfield, Massachusetts
Cambridge, Massachusetts
  (Harvard University — JFK
  School of Government Memorial
  Chapel and Massachusetts
  Institute of Technology)
Providence, Rhode Island
Chapel Hill, North Carolina
Prague, Czechoslovakia
Bratislava, Czechoslovakia
Brno, Czechoslovakia
Berlin, GDR
Dresden (Saxony), GDR
Gorlitz, GDR
Stendal, GDR
Stralsund, GDR
Wittenberg, GDR

Blackpool, England
Moscow, Russia, U.S.S.R.
Nassau, Bahamas
New Orleans, Louisiana
  (Southern Baptist Convention
  Evangelistic Rally)
Boise, Idaho
Spokane, Washington

1983
Oklahoma City, Oklahoma
Orlando, Florida
Sacramento, California
Tacoma, Washington

1984
Anchorage, Alaska
Vancouver, British Columbia,
  Canada
Moscow, Russia, U.S.S.R.
Leningrad, Russia, U.S.S.R.
Novosibirsk, Siberia, U.S.S.R.
Tallinn, Estonia, U.S.S.R.
Seoul, Korea (South)
Liverpool, England
Birmingham, England
Bristol, England
Ipswich, England
Norwich, England
Sunderland, England

1985

Sheffield, England
Arad, Romania
Bucharest, Romania
Cluj-Napoca, Romania
Oradea, Romania
Sibiu, Romania
Suceava, Romania
Timisoara, Romania
Budapest, Hungary
Pecs, Hungary
Hartford, Connecticut
Fort Lauderdale, Florida
Anaheim, California

1986

Paris, France
Washington, D.C.
Tallahassee, Florida

1987

Columbia, South Carolina
Denver, Colorado
Cheyenne, Wyoming
Billings, Montana
Fargo, North Dakota
Sioux Falls, South Dakota
Helsinki, Finland

1988

Kiev, Ukraine, U.S.S.R.
Moscow, Russia, U.S.S.R.
Zagorsk, Russia, U.S.S.R.
Buffalo, New York
Rochester, New York
Hamilton, Ontario, Canada
Beijing, People's Republic of China
Guangzhou, People's Republic of China
Shanghai, People's Republic of China
Hyaiyin, People's Republic of China
Nanjing, People's Republic of China

Preaching in Romania in September 1985.

CHARLOTTE OBSERVER FILE PHOTO

Billy Graham in Peking, China, April 1988.

1989

Budapest, Hungary
Great Britain
London, England
Livelink Centers, Great Britain
Little Rock, Arkansas
Syracuse, New York

Billy Graham during a visit to
Moscow's Russian Orthodox
Patriarchal Cathedral in May 1982.

AP PHOTO

1990s

1990
Albany, New York
Uniondale (Long Island), New York
Berlin, West Germany
Hong Kong
Montreal, Quebec, Canada

1991
Edinburgh, Scotland
Glasgow, Scotland
Aberdeen, Scotland
Buenos Aires, Argentina
East Rutherford, New Jersey
New York City, New York
Seattle, Washington
Tacoma, Washington

1992
Moscow, Russia
Philadelphia, Pennsylvania
Portland, Oregon
Pyongyang, North Korea

Billy Graham with Kim Il Sung in 1994.

AP PHOTO

Billy Graham with Argentina President Carlos Menem in 1991.

AP PHOTO

Billy Graham with Johnny Cash.

AP PHOTO

Billy Graham

1993
Essen, Germany
Pittsburgh, Pennsylvania
Columbus, Ohio

1994
Cleveland, Ohio
Atlanta, Georgia
Beijing, People's Republic of China
Pyongyang, North Korea
Tokyo, Japan

1995
Sacramento, California
San Juan, Puerto Rico
Toronto, Ontario, Canada

1996
Charlotte, North Carolina
Minneapolis/St. Paul, Minnesota

1997
San Antonio, Texas
Oakland, California
San Francisco, California
San Jose, California

1998
Ottawa, Ontario, Canada
Tampa, Florida

1999
Indianapolis, Indiana
St. Louis, Missouri

Billy Graham in Berlin 1990.

AP PHOTO

A Graham crusade in Budapest, Hungary.

Worshippers rejoice during the Greater New York Billy Graham Crusade at Flushing Meadows Corona Park.

2000s

2000
Jacksonville, Florida
Nashville, Tennessee

2001
Fresno, California
Louisville, Kentucky

2002
Cincinnati, Ohio
Dallas/Fort Worth, Texas

Graham in prayer.

KEITH MYERS/THE KANSAS CITY STAR

Graham at the Kansas City crusade in 2004

DAVID EULITT/THE KANSAS CITY STAR

124

TODD SUMLIN/THE CHARLOTTE OBSERVER

Franklin Graham helps his father Billy Graham to a podium in 2005.

TODD SUMLIN/THE CHARLOTTE OBSERVER

Rev. Billy Graham (seated in pulpit) speaks to the 80,000 people on hand for the Greater New York Billy Graham Crusade at Flushing Meadows Corona Park June 25, 2005.

2003
Oklahoma City, Oklahoma
San Diego, California

2004
Kansas City, Missouri

2005
New York, New York

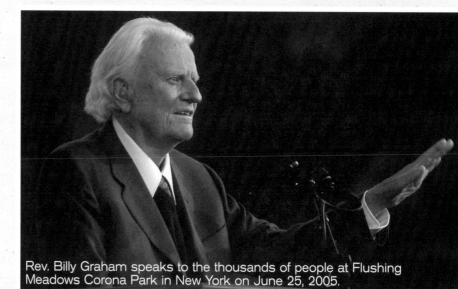

Rev. Billy Graham speaks to the thousands of people at Flushing Meadows Corona Park in New York on June 25, 2005.

TODD SUMLIN/THE CHARLOTTE OBSERVER

TODD SUMLIN/THE CHARLOTTE OBSERVER

Franklin and Billy Graham in 2005.

Franklin Graham holds his granddaughter C.J. Graham during a prayer.

TODD SUMLIN/THE CHARLOTTE OBSERVER

ON THIS CRUSADE STAGE ...

Billy Graham was the magnet that drew millions to his crusades over the decades, all over the world. But those who flocked to stadiums, arenas and parks always heard more than a sermon when they took their seats. It was a Graham crusade tradition to share music and messages from some of the world's best-known singers, politicians and other public personalities. Among the many public figures who shared their voices, faith and stardom over the years:

Singer and movie star Ethel Waters; TV and movie cowboys Roy Rogers and Dale Evans; former-teen-idol-turned-devout-Christian Pat Boone and his singing daughter Debbie; actress and singer Norma Zimmer, who performed with Lawrence Welk and was quite popular in the 1950s; actor Jim Caviezel, who played Jesus in Mel Gibson's controversial hit movie, *The Passion*

Roy Rogers and Dale Evans

AP PHOTO/KEVORK DJANSEZIAN, FILE

Ricky Skaggs

LAURA MUELLER/THE CHARLOTTE OBSERVER

CeCe Winans

CHARLOTTE OBSERVER FILE PHOTO

Jim Caviezel

AP PHOTO/STEFANO PALTERA

Kirk Franklin

CHARLOTTE OBSERVER FILE PHOTO

Pat Boone

AP PHOTO/TODD PLITT

Jars of Clay

CHARLOTTE OBSERVER FILE PHOTO

CHARLOTTE OBSERVER FILE PHOTO

Steven Curtis Chapman

Point of Grace

CHARLOTTE OBSERVER FILE PHOTO

Michael Reagan

PAUL TOPLE/AKRON BEACON JOURNAL

of the Christ; Christian and pop singer Amy Grant; country music legends Johnny and June Carter Cash, Charlie Daniels and Ricky Skaggs; Christian singers Michael W. Smith, Gaither Vocal Band, dc Talk, Jars of Clay, Sandi Patty, Third Day, CeCe Winans, The Cathedrals, The Blackwood Brothers, Andre Crouch, Kirk Franklin, Point of Grace, Steven Curtis Chapman and Kathy Troccoli; and opera star Kathleen Battle.

In each town, the ministry would also invite a mayor, senator or other public official to the podium to speak. Among the political figures who commanded the podium: Chuck Colson, the former Richard Nixon aide who became a prison evangelist; the two George Bushes, before they were president; and Michael Reagan, son of President Ronald Reagan.

But — before Graham stepped up to preach at least — it was usually the hometown sports hero who drew the biggest cheers. Among the athletes who appeared over the decades were NASCAR drivers Jeff Gordon and Michael Waltrip, NFL stars Reggie White, Deion Sanders, Anthony Munoz and Kurt Warner; and popular NFL coach Tony Dungy.

Jesus said:

"I am the Way, the Truth, and the Life"

John 14:6

THE WORK WILL LIVE ON

At the memorial service for his beloved younger brother, Melvin, at Charlotte's Central Church of God in August 2003, Billy Graham told 1,000 mourners he himself was ready to leave this world for something better.

The faith that propelled Graham to lead crusades the world over inspired this unbending belief in an eternal life. It also stirred his conviction that his work will live on long after he's gone, whenever that is.

Dozens of Graham books, his association's films and the popular *Decision* magazine will all sustain the ministry. But for those who want to honor Billy Graham's life, learn more about his continuing work, become a better Christian or simply look back over the years in photos and keepsakes, here are three wonderful places to go:

ASHEVILLE, N.C.

The Billy Graham Training Center in the heart of the Blue

Ridge Mountains devotes 1,500 acres to prayer, solitude, fellowship and learning.

The Cove, as it is known, is located off Interstate 40 not far from the Grahams' home in Montreat. It hosts Christian retreats featuring such prominent speakers as the Grahams' daughter, evangelist Anne Graham Lotz. Among the Bible-based topics:

"Five Signs of a Loving Family" and "Growing Up To Be Like Jesus."

More than opportunities for study, The Cove also offers a chance to pause beside a country stream, exercise along forest trails, and enjoy good food and fellowship in two inns. There are also camps for youth.

As The Cove's web site has stated: "Just as Jesus found it nec-essary to get away from the crowds and go into the mountains for solitude and prayer, each of us can benefit from some time away in a quiet place where we can meet with God and discover the deeper truths of His word."

As Graham told 1,000 gathered at a 1993 celebration marking the opening of The Cove: "I give God all the glory. The future is as bright as the promises of God."

For more on the Billy Graham Training Center, call (800) 950-2092.

CHARLOTTE, N.C.

When Franklin Graham took over leadership of his father's ministry and decided to move the headquarters from Minneapolis to the Grahams' native Charlotte, this much was certain:

The Billy Graham Evangelistic Association must honor the life and times of the evangelist, and Christian evangelism.

The center, located on 63 wooded acres off Billy Graham Parkway near Charlotte/Douglas International Airport, includes a library filled with Graham memorabilia and other material meant to educate and inspire the thousands who come through each year.

For more on the library write to:

The Billy Graham Evangelistic Association
1 Billy Graham Parkway
Charlotte, NC 28201
You can also visit:
www.billygraham.org

Rev. Graham in 2000.

AP PHOTO/ALAN MARLER

Rev. Graham in 1991.

WHEATON, ILL.

Twenty-five miles west of downtown Chicago, on the campus of his alma mater, lies perhaps the most complete tribute:

The Billy Graham Center offers much for the mind, eye and heart:

A library contains thousands of bound volumes, microforms and electronic research databases on Graham and the evangelical Christian movement, with an emphasis on the 20th Century. This is the place to get lost in the past.

Finally, the center organizes programs and offers scholarships in such areas as prison ministry and ethnic outreach — all meant to continue the work that drives the man for whom this is named.

For more on the Billy Graham Center, write 500 College Ave., Wheaton, Ill., 60187.

A museum celebrates the heritage of evangelism in America, from Sojourner Truth to Billy Sunday. Family photos and personal mementos mark the life of Graham. Included are some of his sermon notes, a look back at his crusades through video and even a baseball from his younger days on the south Charlotte dairy farm.

The Cloud Room depicts the resurrection of Christ and glory of heaven. A chapel offers an opportunity to reflect on everything you've just witnessed.

An archive holds documents chronicling the work of Graham through scrapbooks, videos, CDs and more. There are also collections honoring the legacy of other evangelists, including Charles Colson and Corrie ten Boom.

Rev. Graham at his wife Ruth's funeral.

TODD SUMLIN/THE CHARLOTTE OBSERVER

Rev. Graham at his brother Melvin's funeral.

JOHN D. SIMMONS/THE CHARLOTTE OBSERVER

Rev. Graham accepting the Charlotte Chamber of Commerce's Citizen of the Carolinas Award in 1999.

Graham at home in Montreat in 1997.

BILLY GRAHAM EVANGELISTIC ASSOCIATION

A FINAL THOUGHT

"I know that soon my life will be over. I thank God for it, and for all He has given me in this life. But I look forward to Heaven. I look forward to the reunion with friends and loved ones who have gone on before. I look forward to Heaven's freedom from sorrow and pain. I also look forward to serving God in ways we can't begin to imagine, for the Bible makes it clear that Heaven is not a place of idleness. And most of all, I look forward to seeing Christ and bowing before Him in praise and gratitude for all He has done for us, and for using me on this earth by His grace — just as I am."

— *Billy Graham, 1997*

CHRISTOPHER A. RECORD/THE CHARLOTTE OBSERVER

ELMER HORTON/THE CHARLOTTE OBSERVER

DIEDRA LAIRD/THE CHARLOTTE OBSERVER